MIRA MANGA

THE STORY OF THE COMPANY THAT CAME BEFORE

MIRA MANGA

HarperCollins*Publishers*
1 London Bridge Street
London SE1 9GF
WilliamCollinsBooks.com

First published by Lush Handwritten 2013

Text © Cosmetic Warriors Ltd
Artwork credits on page 142

10 9 8 7 6 5 4 3 2 1

The authors assert their moral right to be identified as the authors of this work.

All rights reserved. No parts of this publication may be reproduced, stored in a retrieval system, or transmitted, in any form or by any means, electronic, mechanical, photocopying, recording, or otherwise, without the prior permission of the publishers

A catalogue record for this book is available from the British Library

Library of Congress Cataloging-in-Publication Data has been applied for

ISBN 978-0-00-878954-1

PLU 220600

Written by Mira Manga
Art Direction: Clive Holmes Studios, Suzie Hackney and Julia Lawrence
Artworking: Clive Holmes Studios and Julia Lawrence
Project editor for LUSH: Matt Fairhall
Project editor for HarperCollins*Publishers*: Caitlin Doyle
Proofreader: Helena Caldon
Production controller: Alan Cracknell

All reasonable efforts have been made by the proprietors and publishers to trace the copyright owners of the material quoted in this book and of any images reproduced in this book. In the event that the proprietors or publishers are notified of mistakes or omissions by copyright owners after publication, we will endeavour to rectify the position accordingly for any subsequent printing.

Printed in Italy

Printed on 100% recycled paper with vegetable-based inks

A number of photographs have been taken from our Cosmetics to Go archives. They have been carefully restored and we hope that if you spot yourself in one, it brings back many happy memories.

Any third party trademarks in this book are owned by the relevant third parties unless otherwise expressly stated. The individuals mentioned or featured in this book do not have any connection or association with this book or its authors, and may not at any time have had any connection with this book, Cosmetics to Go, Lush or their respective products or brands.

This is a 2nd edition history of the work of Cosmetics to Go, which traded from 1988 to 1994. It has been revised and edited to respect international, generational and cultural sensitivities, reflecting the more inclusive and compassionate values of today. When viewed through the lens of a modern reader, the branding of some of the Cosmetics to Go ranges may be viewed as cultural appropriation. However, we believe it's important to tell the story of this 1980s company honestly, acknowledging the context of its time, while recognising how much modern culture has evolved since then.

This book contains FSC™ certified paper and other controlled sources to ensure responsible forest management.

For more information visit: www.harpercollins.co.uk/green

*'I think you can say the products
were well and truly tested and
so were the humans!'*

Jeff Osment
Cosmetics to Go Video Producer

Dedicated to my father, Paul. My best friend, my biggest supporter, and my rock. I miss you.

With thanks to Mark, for trusting me to tell this story.

In memory of Clive Holmes, who was invaluable to the original Cosmetics to Go team and to the making of this book.

The Cosmetics to Go team, 1988

Contents

Trouble up the Mountain 13
In the Beginning 14
The Body Shop 16
Making it Up 17
Some Banana Drama 18
Africa Companion 20
The Perfect Parcel 22
Mark & Mo 24
Liz 25
Rowena 26
Helen 27
Letters, Logos, Launch! 28
Khufu 31
Stan Krysztal 32
The Invention of the Shampoo Bar .. 35
Kaleidosoaps 36
Introducing Miriam and Ben, Son of Miriam ... 41
The Invention of the Bath Bomb 42
Keeping Things Fresh 44
Hop Along to the Herb King 48
Botanomancy 50
You Spin Me Right Round 52
CHS... The Catalogue Vision 54
Fighting Animal Testing 58
The Assisi Project 60
Tested on Humans 61
Baby Revels 62
Below Zero 64
Companions 66
Forces Favourites 68
Gigaku 70

Ginger 72
To Know Me Is To Love Me 74
Hollyhocks 76
Superheroes 78
It's All About You 80
Something Borrowed, Something Blue 83
Team Cosmetics to Go 84
The Ten Company Rules 86
Christmas to Go 88
Looking After the People 90
The Factory 92
Factory Tours 94
CTG At the Clothes Show Live 96
CTG on TV 98
Read All About It 102
Setting Up A Local Shop! 104
Cosmetics to Global 106
Don't 'Bovver' With Boots 108
Sea Level 109
Strandlooper 110
Pure Luxury 111
The Ultimate Bathing Experience... 114
Neroli 116
DANGER! The Summer Sale 119
What Next? 122
The Final Clothes Show 123
A Christmas Present 124
Cosmetics to Go Have Gone 126
The Grand Finale: Fizz, Fireworks & Friends .. 130
Credits 142
Thank You 143

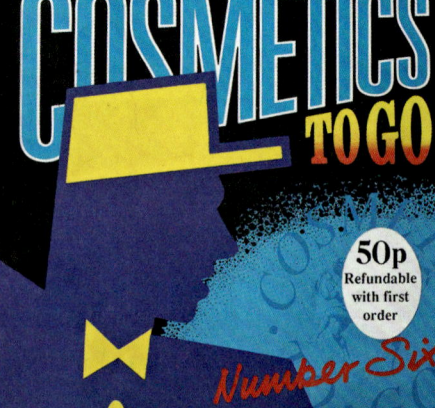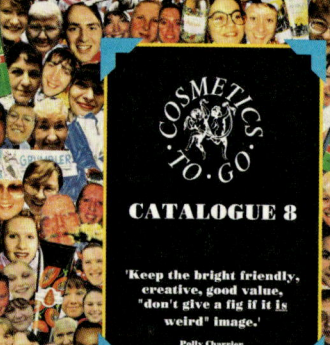

The Cosmetics to Go team taking product testing to the extreme as they trek up the mountain

Trouble up the Mountain

Rowena stood shivering in the cold. Snow was falling fast, clogging her eyelashes while her breath made wispy trails in the freezing air. Yesterday had seen her friend and colleague Susannah stretchered down the mountain suffering from severe altitude sickness.

Rowena had tucked a sleeping bag closely around her friend as the porters tied her to the stretcher frame to secure her on the bumpy ride down. She couldn't forget Susannah looking into her eyes and asking, 'Will I be OK?'

Now, on the final day of the trek and just a short distance from the summit, Uhuru Peak, only two members of the film crew from the sixteen-strong party had actually made it to Gilman's Point, a significant milestone on the rim of Kibo Crater, high on the slopes of mighty Mount Kilimanjaro.

The rest of the crew had peeled off and turned back through fatigue or sickness. Jeff, the director, had collapsed unceremoniously a mere three hundred yards from success.

The journey had been plagued with bad luck, from having to haggle at every stage with porters, to a punishing filming schedule, to the torrential showers that had completely drenched the party as they trudged through the rainforest.

Rowena had headed back to the huts from where the party had departed at midnight. They had hoped to arrive at Gilman's Point in time to see dawn break over Tanzania. When the shortness of breath and dizziness had hit, there was no way she could continue and she had returned to the base at the bottom of the Kibo volcanic cone, reuniting with her fallen comrades.

It was the final frustration of a fiasco of a journey, and it was the end of the road for Rowena in more ways than one. Finding her backpack she pulled out the pad where she had been writing her daily journal. Determined to write a resignation letter, because she was cold with a poorly tummy and never wanted to be tempted to do anything so daft again, she flicked through her notes to find a blank page. Ready to author a raging diatribe ending in a 'Goodbye forever!' to Cosmetics to Go, she put pen to paper and started scribbling. The pen scratched futilely at the page, leaving no marks. The ink was frozen...

'I don't believe it!'

In the Beginning...

The company destined to take centre stage as a gamechanger in the world of cosmetics had been stuck in rehearsals for too long, eagerly awaiting the moment the curtain would rise and their creativity could finally take the spotlight...

Constantine & Weir was a young company that thrived on experimentation and creativity, formed in 1976 by the late beautician Liz Weir and herbalist hair doctor from the forest, Mark Constantine. They first met while working as freelancers at a local hair salon in Poole, in Dorset. They got on well, both personally and professionally. Both were interested in natural beauty products and were quietly ambitious, too.

When Liz's contract came up for renewal they decided to strike out on their own. The first steps towards partnership occurred when Mark found a property in Parkstone that had three treatment rooms. He invited her to come and take a look with him. These rooms were not where they would end up, but they did galvanise their plans to go into business together. Liz would sell her Mini to gather funds, but Mark needed to find a way to get some cash for his contribution.

Mark Constantine and Liz Weir

He had a small operation making herbal hair products with a few local clients, including herbalists and salons. Obsessed with using natural ingredients and their effects on the scalp and skin, he would research and source the most effective herbs. In the evenings at home, after his wife Mo arrived back from work, they would concoct batches of products made to their own recipes.

Trying to make a living, Mark read about a natural beauty cosmetics shop in Brighton called The Body Shop™. He got in touch and made an appointment. It was here that he discovered incipient entrepreneur Anita Roddick, a one-woman whirlwind full of excitement and energy. He was dazzled by Anita and delighted when she fell in love with his offering and placed an order for £1,200 on the spot.

This first order gave him the lump sum that he needed to invest with Liz to get their treatment rooms. Together they found a property at 29 High Street, in Poole, and set up the Herbal Hair Clinic. The products used in the clinic were all made by Mark and Mo.

Liz would perform the beauty treatments, while Mark carried out hair and scalp consultations. The number of customers coming to their tiny rooms was modest and money was tight at first. The Body Shop was to remain a loyal customer and the relationship grew.

The Body Shop

The Body Shop went on to become the phenomenon of the 1980s, capturing the public's imagination. The company burst onto the scene, a breath of fresh air in the established and conventional cosmetics industry, and quickly became a successful player in its own right.

Mark and Anita

The Body Shop exuded a welcoming, friendly atmosphere miles away from the traditional concession-style beauty counters. Fun items like bath beads and bright lip-glosses were sold, and you could bring in your bottles for a refill once you were done, and see them filled in the store. This practical take on cutting down on packaging excited Mark.

Originally, to stock her shop Anita had been buying leftover products from contract cosmetic manufacturers, but now she was able to source completely original creations.

Behind the scenes, Constantine & Weir started to provide The Body Shop with what were to become some of their best-selling products; Cocoa Butter Hand and Body Lotion, Ice Blue Shampoo and Peppermint Foot Lotion, introducing Anita to the concept of aromatherapy.

The Body Shop was expanding so fast that Constantine & Weir had to adapt quickly to match the demand for products. Production increased at lightning speed. Containers of one gallon soon became twenty-five litres, they became two hundred kilos and finally the mighty Palletcons arrived – a container atop a pallet that you would attach a nozzle to and pump a whole tonne of product into!

Fecund and free in their creativity, Mark, Mo, Liz, Rowena and Helen, the inventors and wizards that populated the labs, would enthusiastically whip up mysterious and extraordinary products at an explosive pace. Spurred on by their pioneering achievements (more on these later!), the creative cosmeticians invented new categories of product that had never previously existed in the world of bathing projects.

These new inventions would be put before Anita, who would decide whether or not to accept them into The Body Shop range.

The Classics   Herbal Hair Colour   Aromatherapy

Making it Up

Constantine & Weir had other customers besides The Body Shop. Its own hair salon, run from the company's property on Poole High Street, sold the eponymously-named range 29½ and they also manufactured bespoke ranges for local Poole hairdressing salons **Scissors and Level.**

There was also a long list of named brands that became customers. The Trichology Centre, John Frieda, Michael John, Hive & Herb and Czech & Speake all sold hair-care lines developed and manufactured by the team.

At this time The Body Shop was the fastest-growing cosmetic company in the world, ordering massive amounts of products that dwarfed the orders from these smaller companies. They certainly provided the stimulus that allowed Constantine & Weir to develop and explore new product ideas and inventions.

John Frieda

Czech & Speake

Trichology Centre

Scissors

29½

New Society

Hive & Herb

Shades of Paradise

The Body Shop & Making it Up | 17

Some Banana Drama

Banana Republic, a mail-order clothing company owned by travelling couple Mel and Patricia Ziegler, had impressed members of Constantine & Weir. The quirky catalogue was filled with airbrushed pictures illustrating each item and had charmed the team, who all bought clothes from it and spent time admiring the clothing descriptions and travel stories.

'*That was the inspiration. They created airbrush illustrations for every single item of clothing. She (Patricia) was an illustrator and he (Mel) was a writer. It's so special, I used to buy all this stuff and wear it.*'

Mark

'*We all loved Banana Republic. We used to place orders all the time. There was forever something turning up from there...*'

Rowena

Rowena loved Banana Republic so much that she, along with colleagues Stephen Smalls and Sue Sievers, decided to create a cosmetics range to pitch to them. This range would become known as the Africa Companion, and was designed to complement Banana Republic's iconic safari-themed style, aligning with its adventurous aesthetic.

Mark, however, was not convinced, and politely advised his colleagues to concentrate on their day jobs. Despite his misgivings, Rowena and her colleagues secretly continued to develop their idea.

They often waited until most people had left for the day and would work surreptitiously into the night. If Mark happened to wander past, they would quickly sweep all the products off the benches and frantically try to waft any incriminating scents away. They had chosen a particularly distinctive melon scent for this range and they knew its unusual smell could tip him off to their clandestine activities.

On the rare occasion that Mark caught a glimpse of what they were up to, they would hear him booming:

> *What are you doing?! Pack it in whatever it is!*

Thankfully for us, they totally ignored him and continued to design the beautiful Africa Companion range.

Some Banana Drama

Africa Companion

The complete Africa Companion range included sunscreens, moisturisers, a body wash that could wash your clothes as well as you, a lip balm and a mosquito repellent.

Rowena found some scrim – a coarse wheat-coloured fabric – in her local hardware shop and designed a travel pouch. The kit was beautifully presented all ready to wrap up and pop into your suitcase.

Shortly afterwards, during a conference in Heathrow, Mark was called to the front desk, allowing him to slip out of proceedings with his colleague Karl Bygrave in tow. It was there that they discovered an unexpected package was waiting for him.

Back in the hotel room, they were surprised upon opening the parcel to find the beautifully presented Africa Companion set. Each item featured a luggage-tag-style label describing how to use the products and how to pronounce their names.

The team had outdone themselves and went the extra mile by including a special bar of white chocolate. The original wrapping paper had been removed and was replaced with an African-themed label showing pictures of elephants and jokingly inscribed, 'Made with 100% elephant milk.'

He called Rowena, congratulated her and her team and agreed they could pitch their inventions to Banana Republic. She sent off the Africa Companion wrap for the attention of Mel and Patricia Ziegler, and waited to hear back.

And waited… and waited.

The products and concept were perfect for Banana Republic, but the timing may have been slightly off. Mel and Patricia were in talks to sell their company to The Gap, and we wonder if these takeover wranglings may have overshadowed the arrival of this business opportunity. Whatever the reason, they said no. Everyone was disappointed.

All that hard work had given the team an idea. They wanted to sell their own ranges but did not want to step on The Body Shop's toes, as it was still their biggest customer. The Body Shop was unable to go into the mail-order business, as this could have upset their franchisees. Constantine & Weir, however, manufacturing all their own products, were in a great

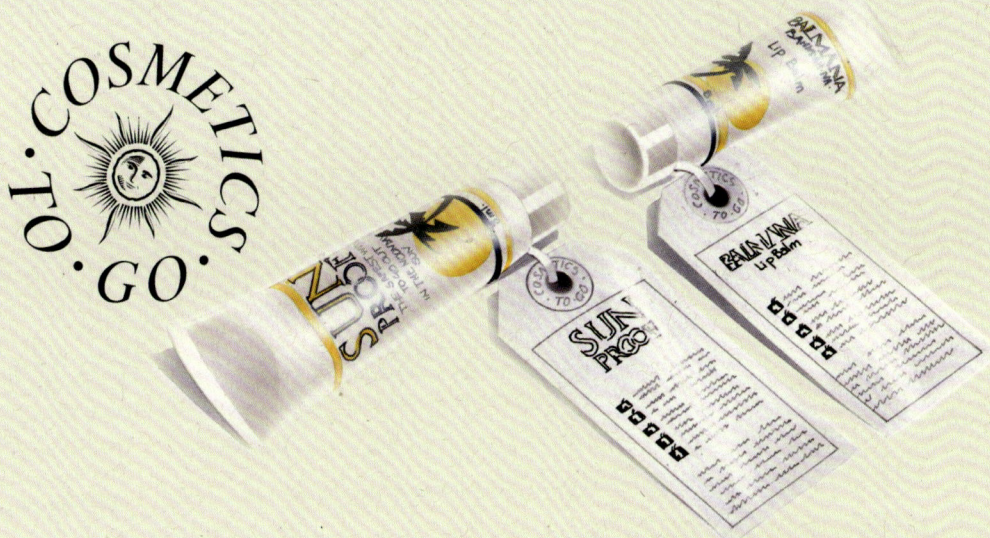

position to produce their own catalogue-based mail-order business.

George Davis, a brilliant retail entrepreneur, had recently taken over the shops of a traditional suit maker called Hepworth and turned them into Next, a chain of clothing stores that became very popular. He had then taken Grattans, an established catalogue company, and turned that into Next Direct, with similar results. Mail order was suddenly sexy and the great British public were switching on to buying through catalogues. The idea was formed that Constantine & Weir could launch their own mail-order business selling their own cosmetics and strike out independently. This would be a huge change.

The pages of a catalogue would provide opportunities for creativity to shine through, not to mention that it would allow them to control every aspect of their business with nothing standing in the way of getting the products directly to customers.

The idea was mooted and discussed within the business. In those days, twenty-eight days delivery was standard, and if it didn't fit or there was a mistake with your order, it would take another twenty-eight days to get your money back or your replacement.

If they were going to do a mail-order company it was decided it would be speedy, reliable, fun and completely blow other companies of its ilk out of the water. As Karl commented:

'We felt that mail order was ripe for a revolution because it was full of ordinary goods. What we had was something different and never-before seen.'

Cosmetics to Go opened to great public acclaim, and despite all the efforts not to upset Anita, within a few years The Body Shop had offered nine million pounds, to be paid over three years, to take ownership of a number of Constantine & Weir's product formulas and manufacturing techniques.

The only caveat of this agreement was that Constantine & Weir had to promise not to open any retail outlets, except the shop at 29 High Street, Poole, that would be in direct competition with The Body Shop.

Africa Companion | 21

The Perfect Parcel

With a brand new company, image was key. The parcel arriving at a customer's door was the perfect opportunity to show how special and unique this fledgling company was.

Mark asked Rowena to design the perfect parcel. If the company was going to do mail order it would have to be something that totally stood out from the rest of the companies out there. A vessel for all the extraordinary Cosmetics to Go products to arrive in that would turn heads and make people take notice.

Rowena tried quite a few box designs and presented them. Each time Mark would look unimpressed, with a curl of the lip and a shake of the head, nevertheless Rowena persisted. Experimenting with packaging and different boxes, she presented her efforts time and time again. Rowena has always been renowned for her sunny and cheery disposition, but after numerous presentations and rejections it would be fair to say she was at the end of her tether. Each time she showed him what she had come up with he would complain that it wasn't fun enough.

One particular day, Mark rejected the package that she was showing him and told her that it wasn't good enough and she needed to be creating something really, really exciting.

'You want a parcel, I'll give you a parcel!'

Eventually, she came up with a winning design when she delivered a brightly decorated parcel, festooned with stamps and stickers to look like a well-travelled suitcase. The brown-paper package was lovingly tied up with string and sealed with a wax stamp. Inside the box were products nestled in shredded paper with sweets and chocolate treats alongside them.

Finally Mark was pleased. In fact, more than pleased – he was delighted. The package was eye-catching, colourful and completely different to any parcel you would receive from any other mail-order company. The attention to detail in the product, packaging, tags and the look of the parcel won him over.

With the products ready, a snappy company name and an exciting parcel that you just couldn't wait to rip open, this show was ready to roll.

The Perfect Parcel | 23

Mark & Mo

Mark grew up and went to school in the town of Weymouth, and it was here that he met Mo. Mo first heard about 'Connie' from her younger sister, who came home talking about a high-spirited young man who'd been flirting with her at school. When Mo finally met this infamous tearaway at an all-night party, she took a look and thought, 'He doesn't seem that bad at all. I think I can mould something out of that!'

It didn't take long for the two of them to become inseparable. For Mark, life had been chaotic. A rocky time with his mum and stepdad had left him homeless at 16, with his mother telling him, 'You're on your own now.'

With no family to turn to, because his father had abandoned the family when he was only two, Mark was staying with friends whenever he could, but sometimes had to sleep outside in a nearby forest. Mo, on the other hand, came from a more stable home. Her calm and steady presence was an anchor for Mark, and a reassuring foundation in his life. In the evenings, Mo would walk him to the gate of the woods, where he would head off to sleep under the stars.

They married at twenty-one, both certain that they had found the person they wanted to be with forever. Mo used to work in the law courts, and was a shorthand typist by profession. Mark had studied cosmetology and trichology and was a junior hair dresser. Between these two salaries, they were able to get enough money together for rent.

Once qualified, and after he took on a treatment room at a local hairdresser in Poole, Mark and Mo began formulating lotions and creams for his clients. In the evening, they would fill shampoos and creams into jars with a spoon. Mo created labels on a home computer which they would apply by hand.

Their partnership was a perfect fusion of vision and practicality. Mark had the ideas and brokered the deals and contacts, Mo had her own ideas, coming up with blends and inventions alongside him. She had the patience, perseverance and the hands-on skills to turn product ideas into reality.

Looking back, Mark would say that he considered himself one of Mo's greatest achievements, crediting her for 'sorting him out' and saying he wouldn't have done what he'd done without her.

Mark and Mo... ...true young loves... ...together forever

Liz
1952–2020

Although Liz was destined to work alongside Mark in the beauty industry, her destiny did not appear so obvious at first...

As a schoolgirl, Liz had decided to take up the offer of a course in food science and management at Queen Elizabeth's College at the University of London. She was provisionally accepted onto the course, her accommodation was booked and everyone was preparing to wave her off, when she suddenly had an epiphany and turned down the offer.

Liz's decision seemed incomprehensible to some of the community. She was summoned to come and explain her reasoning to the education board in the local magistrate's court.

Liz explained that recently her school's career department had taken her class on a trip to Chichester College. Seeing the treatments and therapies first hand had inspired her to become a beauty therapist.

The panel were not happy with this revelation and over the next few hours tried to persuade her to think about a different university course. Liz was politely insistent and managed to convince them that she had made up her mind. At this point it emerged that the wife of one of the panel members ran a beauty therapy course. Impressed by Liz's tenacity, he spoke to his wife that same day. This was on a Friday. On Monday Liz started at the beauty college.

After she had successfully completed her course, she was pleasantly surprised to receive a slew of job offers. Estée Lauder and DuBois & Russell were both interested in her, but she went for one of two offers from a small beauty company called Louis Marcel.

This company sourced and trained beauty therapists to become franchise owners. For her twenty-first birthday, her father paid for the franchise and gave her the key to her own business. It was here, within a month of opening her first beauty room in Poole at a Marc Young hairdressing salon, that she would serendipitously meet a trichologist called Mark. Thanks to Liz's determination to follow the beauty route, food science's loss was our gain!

Rowena

Ever since Rowena was a little girl, she enjoyed playing with make-up and visiting beauty counters.

Some of Rowena's fondest childhood memories are of getting the bus into Northampton on Saturdays and eagerly spending all her pocket money on make-up, rings and nail varnish. Woolworths was her favourite as they sold all the affordable and exciting kinds of make-up that she loved.

Rowena collected lipsticks in every possible shade; her mum and her mum's friends donated most of these to her. They all contributed to her growing hoard and she ended up with quite a collection. She loved carefully scooping out the remaining lipsticks and mashing different colours together to make her own bespoke shades.

At school, she was a dedicated follower of fashion and beauty. Living close by, she would nip home at lunchtimes to change into different-coloured tights and refresh her make-up. She also had a selection of wigs to choose from so she could change her appearance dramatically whenever she wished. Having fun with cosmetics was her way of life and totally immersive.

It was only natural then that following school, and after a brief time as a window dresser, she would take a course in beauty therapy. Here began her love affair with colour cosmetics, which would flourish and evolve into a fulfilling lifelong career.

Once qualified, she heard about a small company by the seaside that ran therapy rooms and made cosmetics as well. Liz and Mark had been looking for someone to join the team...

Helen

Helen used to be a client of Liz's at their Herbal Hair and Beauty Clinic. She had first come to them as she was suffering from eczema on her face. She wanted a herbal solution instead of the conventional steroid creams that were often prescribed. After a consultation, Liz gave her a hand-made honey beeswax and jojoba oil* cleanser to use. Helen used this every day and was pleased with the results. She became a fan of the products and the beauty treatments too.

When Helen saw an advert in the *Dorset Echo* asking for someone to help Mark making products she jumped at the opportunity and applied for an interview.

Helen's background seemed perfect. She had spent time working in scientific labs but also had worked for the Institute of Terrestrial Ecology on carrying out research on various crops. This gave her a great mixture of knowledge of the benefits of natural ingredients as well as the scientific savvy to mix formulas.

Helen went to Mark's house for her interview and was shown into his kitchen where all the products were developed. Once in conversation, Mark discovered her love of botany and her chemistry know-how. After she described how her horse-riding hobby required her to groom and muck out a stable of four horses she got the job. She took to it quickly, beginning by helping to develop the products and moving on to make her own inventions.

Helen

*This was an early incarnation of a cleanser that Helen has used for over thirty years..! It still appears in Lush as Ultrabland cleanser.

Sending out the first catalogues!

Rowena takes some orders

Letters, Logos, Launch!

Cosmetics to Go was born in a leap year on the 29 February 1988. **The first catalogue** was bursting with exciting inventions and products, as well as many different logos jostling for attention.

The Running Man reflected the personal touch and speedy deliveries that the company were to become known for. His look was based on a hotel bellboy and he was usually pictured with a parcel in hand rushing to his next destination.

The ubiquitous **Cosmetics to Go circular stamp** was used on every parcel that went out. Each of the product ranges had a unique logo. These were represented by their own identifying image inside the circle. See how many different range logos you can spot in this book, we have lost count!

The cheerful cherubs regularly appeared in the company's branding, too. They particularly flocked to the Baby Revels pages (see pages 62–63) but were always present fluttering about the pages.

Postie fills his vans to get our parcels on their way

Parcels ready to go...

28 | Cosmetics to Go

Marcia and Emma opening mail

Logging orders into the computer

Orders keep coming! Helen takes more calls

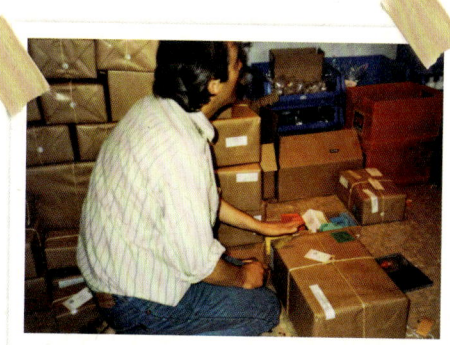
Mark sits with the parcels

COSMETICS BY POST

Tube travel from Dorset

SUSAN OWENS finds a chemist mixing new, needed, natural potions

MARK CONSTANTINE has never been on the centre court in the cosmetic world. He is an innovative chemist who, in a small laboratory in Poole, Dorset, blends intractable ingredients for major manufacturers.

These giants hold him in the highest regard. Though they set him rigid parameters he always tries to expand them. Camomile and jojoba are old hat to Constantine, who now prefers extracts from an African plant called bamyasi to cool and heal sun-tired skins, quince seed for rich lathering shaving creams, and Irish moss to treat very dry hair.

Constantine trained as a trichologist in London, and always offered alternative hair treatments to clients who visited him in Poole. But he had no outlet for the unorthodox elixirs he enjoyed making.

Then 10 years ago, Anita Roddick of Body Shop fame found that her first shop in Brighton had shelves full of bottles she could not afford to fill at the time. Here was Constantine's perfect opportunity. Her ideal of selling only naturally-based products matched his enthusiasm for creating them. Because of Constantine's skills, the Body Shop blazed a trail through the cosmetic world.

He still makes many of their products, but he opens the lines tomorrow for a venture of his own, Cosmetics To Go. Yes, beauty by mail order.

He had found that too many of the new ingredients he turned up weren't acceptable to the shampoo sheiks and face-cream countesses he worked for.

'Even the Body Shop has become conservative,' he says. 'They don't produce as many new products as they did five years ago.' As a result, the shelves in his laboratory are piled high with products that no one, save his loyal staff of 47, ever uses. 'It frustrated the staff that these products weren't produced commercially. But I backed off. It wasn't so long ago that I worked from two rooms in the High Street, and had a healthy overdraft.'

Then, three years ago, when he was in the north of England to give a lecture to the cosmetic industry, he received through the post at his hotel a small package. It contained a hessian wrapper which unrolled to show six products stashed in compartments, a kit designed for a holiday in the sun.

The label said 'Complete Africa Companion' and the six tubes contained sunscreens (three), Africa Wash, which cleanses face, hair and clothes in fresh or salt water, a lip balm and body cream. Each product carried a self-explanatory tag and list of ingredients.

'My staff had sent it,' says Constantine. 'They wanted to overcome my reluctance to producing cosmetics commercially. They tempted me with this surprise package, and I was seduced.'

Tomorrow, Cosmetics To Go will answer on Freephone 0800 373 366. Callers can ask for the free glossy catalogue.

Asked how this compares with the Next mail-order, Constantine says the marketing is the same. 'The catalogue is detailed, the products accurately illustrated. My girls were rather miffed to discover that the Next telephone operators all had six months' training, and chewing-gum exercises to improve their enunciation. I was looking for girls with a nice personality. We trained them by ringing them up ourselves. We did it every five minutes for weeks. We think they're word perfect without the chewing gum.'

This take-out beauty is inexpensive, and comprises six ranges within the catalogue. All the products are made without animal testing. Instead, Constantine has pushed the development of the Assisi Test, a technique which should eventually put an end to trying out ingredients on animals. 'We apply a cosmetic to a culture of human cells and measure the effect. It's the first time this has been achieved. Considerably kinder than spraying a solution into the eyes of rabbits.'

This new safety test, now standard for Cosmetics To Go, was introduced because Constantine wanted to do a baby range, with soaps, talcs, waterproof creams and moisuriser. Helen Ambrosen, who developed the range with hundreds of mothers with pre-school children, says the £1.50 moisturiser is not for daily use. 'Babies develop dry skins as a result of irritating clothes, or sheets, or a change in climate.

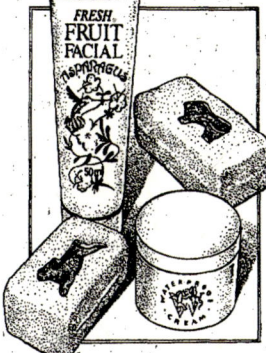

Asparagus face mask, £2.50; 'sand bar' soap, £1.75; waterproof cream to prevent nappy rash, £1.75; 'rub a dub scrub' for skin, £1.75.

You simply rub the cream between your hands to warm it, then slide your hands over those dry areas. Cheeks are very vulnerable.'

Among adults' products are a complete range for men, with pyramid razor-blade sharpener and an innovative line-up of soaps including one for the face that is pliable (patent pending), True Grit for grubby hands and Peach Melba for sensitive facial skin. Should you telephone your order for an Asparagus Fruit Facial Mask (£2.50), it will be made up for you and despatched with a 'use by' date, because the active enzymes in the mask lose their effectiveness in time.

Constantine has even taken the risk of making colour cosmetics, defying sceptics who say you cannot reproduce the exact colours in a catalogue. Rowena Hofbauer, who developed the line, worked side by side with the printers using computer scans to ensure accuracy of colour reproduction.

'What can I say?' says Constantine with steadfast confidence. 'The largest seller of lipsticks in the UK is Avon. They seem to have proved you can sell colour through a brochure.'

■ *Cosmetics To Go is at 29 High Street, Poole, Dorset BH15 1AB.*

Reproduced with permission of the copyright owner. Further reproduction prohibited without permission.

This article by Susan Owens appeared in the Observer *on the day of the launch raving about Cosmetics to Go and printing their Freephone telephone number. Its impact was huge and they received a glut of phone calls and orders through the post as a result. Cosmetics to Go was off!!*

Letters, Logos, Launch! | 29

Khufu

Developing a new product range for men, the team took inspiration from ancient Egypt's rich history and culture. The collection was named after Khufu, the pharaoh who oversaw the building of the Great Pyramid of Giza.

The centrepiece of the range was a large, pyramid-shaped gift box designed to contain the entire collection. A special plinth for a razor and a tiny compass was also included in the set as the team had come across a theory that if you placed a razor blade a third of the way up a pyramid on a North / South axis it would sharpen overnight. Customers were encouraged to write in and let the company know whether their razors had indeed become sharper. Reports that came back were mixed.

A purpose-built pyramid was also constructed in the factory. Water was left beneath it overnight to absorb 'energy' before being used in product formulations.

Every aspect of the Khufu range was influenced by ancient Egypt. The face protector cream was named after Amun, the Great Protector god, while Set was chosen as the name for the clay-based hair fixer.

The Khufu range was named after Egyptian pharaoh King Khufu, who built the Great Pyramid at Giza.

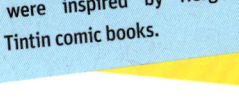

The torchlight illustrations were inspired by Hergé's Tintin comic books.

Stan Krysztal
1905–1992

It became evident with the development of ever more innovative and outlandish items that the company would need a consultant cosmetic chemist to help develop some of the ideas…

The team were delighted to come across the respected Stanislaw Krysztal, a cosmetic chemist renowned for his work on several iconic brands including Mary Quant, Nivea, No 17, Gala and myriad others. Trained in the UK and America in the 1930s after emigrating from Poland, he brought more than forty years' experience to Cosmetics to Go.

Stan was used to working in development facilities that had cost millions of pounds to set up – a very different world from the do-it-yourself-style set up in Poole. After taking a tour of all the facilities, he was very gracious and agreed to join the team.

Helen had always said that she saw developing cosmetics as more of an art than a science, and in Stan they found someone sympathetic to this creative way of working.

He had so much expertise in so many areas that he was to prove invaluable. He was a keen inventor, but was also able to teach the team, sharing his skills and knowledge. He was always eager to try new ideas and methods, advancing his already formidable knowledge. He always liked to know what was going on and would throw himself into exciting new projects, even offering himself as a willing test subject.

Helen recalls a time when Stan expressed an interest in a waxing product that Liz was testing. She kindly offered to show him how it worked and at his nod, quick as a flash, she applied the wax to his arm and ripped it off. 'Oooh! She hurt me!' he yelped, just as shocked at the unexpected sting as by the fact that someone as softly spoken and gentle as Liz could have mischievously caused it!

When he joined Cosmetics to Go, he was already in his late seventies. Luckily for everyone, he didn't believe in retirement. In his time at the company he worked across ranges helping to develop hot soaps, shampoo bars, colour cosmetics and cruelty-free bleach. He also helped the company upscale their production quantities as they grew and taught Rowena how to make colour cosmetics.

In 1992, at the age of 83, Stan passed away. It was testament to his work ethic that even when he was housebound in bed, he was still sending in meticulous memos advising the Cosmetics to Go team on pertinent issues they needed to consider. He bequeathed his library of reference books and formulas to them, and these are treasured.

Stan was proud of his Polish heritage, and he would have been elated to see so many of his countryfolk now working for Lush. His legacy was to live on, not only in the work that Cosmetics to Go continued after his death, but in all future endeavours of the team that had learned so much from him.

Discussions in the lab

Stan and Rowena

Stanislaw Krysztal at work in the CTG labs

> The Inasia Shampoo Bars are brilliant. They are so thick and rich and creamy and lathery and soft and soapy and squidgy.
>
> **Zoë Goodchild**, Guisborough, Cleveland.

> Inasia Shampoo bars are mucho excellento value dough wize...
>
> **Linda Fraser** - Glasgow.

The INASIA name came from Mark and Mo's youngest son Jack, who had been brought to the meeting where the names of the new shampoo bars were being decided. After the grown ups had run out of steam suggesting names, and discussion had descended into dreadful puns and uninspired ideas, Mark leaned down to where his son was playing under the meeting table and said, '*Jack, what shall we call these shampoos?*'

A small voice piped up... '*I not a soap! I a Jack!!*' and he emerged grinning. The adults were bowled over at the cuteness of this turn of phrase. All of a sudden '*I not a soap I a shampoo bar*' became the obvious choice, and the acronym INASIA became the official name of the range.

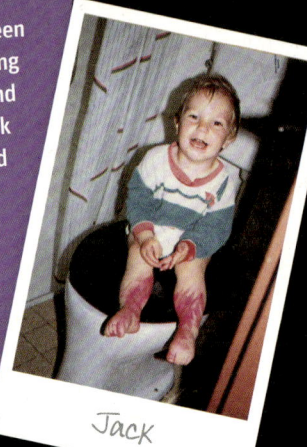

Jack

34 | Cosmetics to Go

The Invention of the Shampoo Bar

One of Cosmetic to Go's proudest moments was the birth of the shampoo bar. A brand-new invention that would revolutionise hair washing all over the country, produce beautiful barnets and save the planet too!

The humble shampoo bar was actually a lucky mistake. Its invention began after Stan showed Mo a new type of soap that he was working on. He had nicknamed it his 'worm soap', so-called because he was playing around with wormy-looking synthetic detergent noodles. He had the idea of using hand presses to squeeze the noodles into shape. Mo joined him in his experiments, but suggested he swap out the synthetic noodles for some surfactant needles.

With the noodles to needles switch in place, the perfectly pressed discs looked great. Sadly, they discovered during testing that they had the wrong consistency of lather for soap. He and Mo were disappointed and puzzled over what to do, until Mark had a look and pointed out that what they had created was not soap at all. They had actually unknowingly invented a brand new product. What they had come up with was a solid shampoo bar. Such is the nature of Mother Invention. She likes to make you think you are heading in one direction and then throws you a curveball.

Each bar was a very hardworking shampoo that acted as a perfect base for all the lovely ingredients that they wanted to deliver gently to the hair and scalp. Once Mo and Stan realised what they had created, the possibilities were limitless.

An Inventor is Born

Although many of the Cosmetics to Go team enjoyed the limelight, Mo preferred operating quietly behind the scenes. She could be found in her shed or in the lab working on ideas that were to become standout products for the company.

During her work with Stan, especially on the development of the soaps and shampoo bars, Mo had a lot of breakthroughs through her experiments. Her method was to start with a simple idea and spend time working with ingredients until she would emerge blinking into the sunlight holding something quite wonderful in her hand.

Cosmetics to Go applied for and won a patent to protect the invention of shampoo bars. There was much celebration when the patent was granted to Stan and Mo.

This official recognition and Mo's growing list of unique products inspired her to proudly write Inventor as her occupation when her new passport arrived.

KALEIDOSOAPS

The soaps had been Mo's passion ever since she had started creating them in her shed for Constantine & Weir. Once Cosmetics to Go was set up she was free to express all the exciting designs she had been storing up and holding onto. Most of the pun-tastic soap names were her ideas too…

There were two methods of making the Cosmetics to Go soaps. The first was a traditional cold method, which the team had explored when they had provided The Body Shop with Elizabethan Wash Balls.

This process required stirring all the ingredients together into a putty-like paste. This allowed heavy ingredients like fruit, pumice or even sand to be added to the mix, leading to imaginative and unexpected combinations. Once mixed, the paste would then be hand-pressed to form solid soap bars.

The True Grit bar was one of these and was named after the gritty, award-winning Western starring John Wayne, because this soap was a toughie. Designed with gardeners, mechanics, builders and anyone who ended up with mucky paws at the end of the day in mind, it needed to be effective. This bar contained pumice to slough off any grime, chlorophyll gave its green

Mo hard at work

Traditional cold method

"Thought you ought to know, my husband - a dairy farmer - has tried every hand cleanser there is, but since trying your True Grit soap he refuses to use anything else and his hands are clean!"
Wife of a dairy farmer.

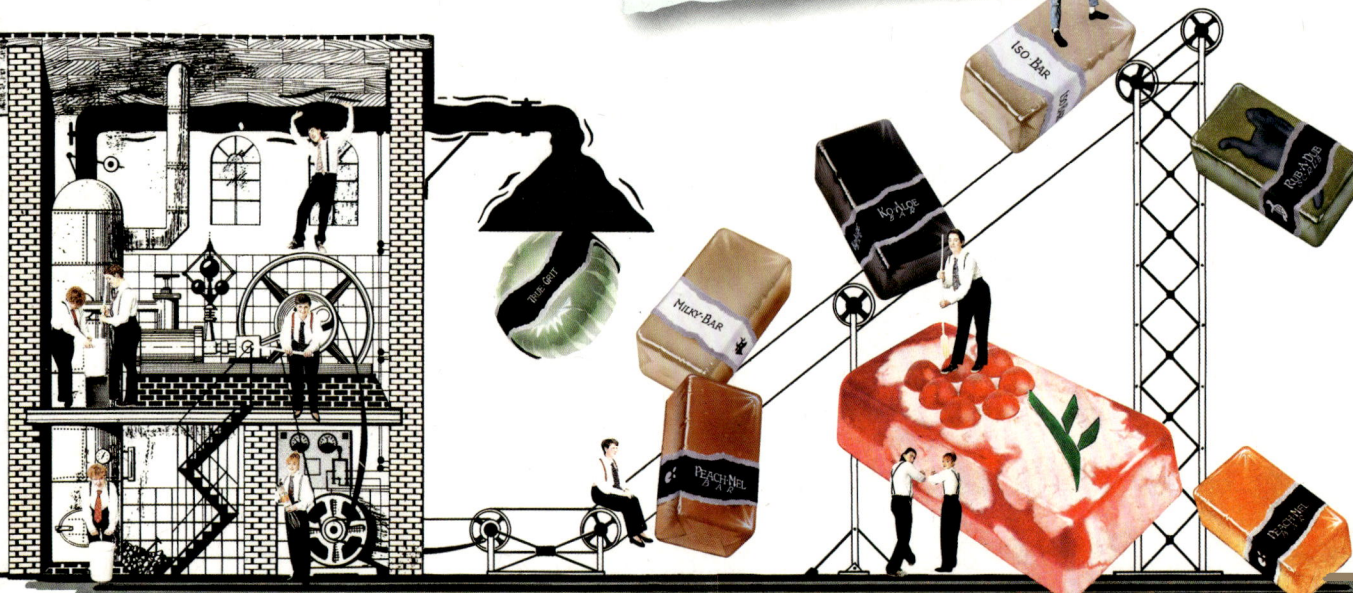

Cosmetics to Go

colour and helped soothe cuts and scratches and an infusion of rosemary also soothed and acted as an antiseptic.

These cold-mix soaps were great for exfoliation. The Peach Mel Bar was named after the delicious Peach Melba dessert and was full of fresh fruit. It contained peaches, pears and apples.

Sandbar started out as a member of the Khufu range. It was a cunning mixture of sand and bananas. The sand provided a bracing exfoliation and the bananas would nourish and moisturise the skin. This bar had a melon fragrance and was adorned with a tiny red lion soap.

The Iso bar was a tingling menthol and spearmint mix that stimulated and invigorated the skin. Iso bar referred to the lines that weather forecasters used to represent atmospheric pressure, so the bar had a frosting over it to make it look icy cold and chilly. A big part of the fun of inventing these soaps was finding fabulous puns that would allow the bar to be described and also end naturally in the word 'bar'.

The second type of soap was made using a hot method. Mo and Stan worked together to develop a liquid soap mix that could be poured into moulds. It was important to keep things colourful and fun, but more than that, they wanted to find a formula that would also hold essential oils, decoctions and various powders that would have beneficial properties.

Honey I Washed the Kids was one of these. It appeared in the later catalogues but didn't really catch on, despite its sweet caramel scent and honeycomb design. Lush would later launch this honey soap, selling freshly cut slices from a large soap round topped with beeswax. It became an instant best seller.

Soaps - are great - Milky bar range but could they be family sized!
A customer who likes King Coconut, Creeper, Serpentine, Myddval...

Kaleidosoaps | 37

Mark Bethell

There was a lot of excitement with all the various inventions emerging from the soap room. It was a constant challenge to keep up the impetus and creativity with even more weird and wonderful products. Through the various experiments and ideas, brand new products such as a foaming soap paper were realised and featured proudly in the catalogues.

To stimulate more creativity, a company-wide competition was held where all the staff were invited to submit their ideas for soap making. This was where the 'Bethell Method' was born.

Employee Mark Bethell, who worked in the factory, decided to enter the competition. Using his past experience as a dental technician, he had a play around with some moulds and experimented with different soap-setting times. He invented a simple layering technique where a bright-coloured soap would be poured into the bottom of a mould and left to harden. Later, another colour would be added to achieve a multi-coloured, 3D-style soap.

He submitted his idea and went off on a sabbatical. Arriving back after seven weeks away in New Zealand and Australia, he was shocked to discover that he had won. Not only that, he was asked to immediately move from the factory to join the soap team. His brief was to develop fifteen more revolutionary ideas in soap.

The Bethell Method was used to great effect in designing a fish family consisting of a brightly coloured Daddy, Mummy and Baby fish. Each one was made with a loop on the back so they could be displayed on the wall in a flying ducks formation.

Some of the more ambitious soaps looked fantastic, but they were time-consuming and expensive to produce. Each layer needed time to cool before the next could be added, and it was tricky to ease the soaps out of the moulds intact.

Despite this, the soap department evolved hugely over time, produced one of the most celebrated and strong product lines, broke a world record and was always producing new, exciting, weird, wonderful and wacky inventions, all in the name of a good wash.

The BIG Soap

Cosmetics to Go burst into the record books with the world's largest soap. It weighed in at 4,629.5 kilos and was taller than Mo, measuring 5ft by 5ft by 6ft. Actor Richard Norton, the resident hunk in Australian soap opera *Home and Away*, did the soap-cutting honours using a chainsaw!

Daddy Fish, Mummy Fish and Baby Fish, or as they were collectively known, The Three Jolly Fish

'SOAPS FOR ALL SEASONS AND REASONS'
Georgina King - Halifax

Kaleidosoaps | 39

Introducing Miriam and Ben, Son of Miriam

A remarkable mother and son team would also emerge from the soap department!

Traditionally each soap was given a clever name, often pun-related and designed to make customers smile. Funny, clever, silly names were always required and many meetings were dominated by people calling out suggestions, making lists of ideas for names, groans and moans at particularly bad puns and wincing when the inspiration was not arriving.

One day at the end of a particularly long meeting, Mo presented a beautiful new product. It was made of ground Spanish almonds, kaolin and glycerine and scented with a lavender essential oil blend. It was a very gentle facial cleanser that didn't lather and produced a delicate almond milk wash when mixed with water.

When asked what it should be called Mo was reluctant to enter into another long name ideas session, so she said, '*Oh I don't know. Call it Miriam!*' and left the room. This off-the-cuff remark was taken at its word and Miriam was born!

Not long after, when the next amazing facial soap came along, packed full of calamine and camomile especially for sensitive and irritated skin, it was decided that it should be known as Big Ben. Big Ben was dubbed the son of Miriam and was scented with the same lavender fragrance.

These two modestly named soaps became renowned for their miraculous healing and soothing properties, were super effective and grew a huge following of loyal customers who adored the effects on their skin.

This tiny family of two was to leave a long legacy, with their descendants appearing as two strong sellers in the Lush range. Indeed, Miriam's new incarnation as Angels on Bare Skin has been a bestselling product worldwide since launch with over 15 million pots sold, equating to more than 1,500 tonnes.

Fresh Farmacy, which is what Ben was renamed, does very well too. Both of these products remain stalwarts of the Lush skincare range more than thirty years later.

The Invention of the Bath Bomb

Cosmetics to Go's fizzing balls of fun were the talk of the town! A strike against boring bath times, these bath bombs wooed even the most recalcitrant bather to make pilgrimage to the tub, where they would oooh! and ahhh! as spheres of sizzling delight were unleashed to effervesce furiously.

Mo and Jeff Brown, the Cosmetics to Go perfumer (more about him on page 74), were discusssing effervescing baths and how they worked. Mo has sensitive skin, so she needed to be sure whatever she bathed in was not going to be too harsh. '*All I want is something that leaves loveliness in the bath and makes my skin feel good,*' she said.

Jeff, who used to work for Beechams, suggested she should get down to the pharmacist and pick up some Alka Seltzer, '*Have a look at how they work,*' he suggested. Alka Seltzer is the famous hangover cure that bursts into bubbles when it's immersed in water, and a household name due to its onomatopoeic '*plink, plink, fizz!*' advertising.

Intrigued, Mo went to investigate and discovered the two effervescing ingredients were sodium bicarbonate and citric acid. It was the reaction of these with water that provided the famous '*fizz*' after the '*plink!*' Disappearing into her inventing shed, she played around testing various recipes until she came up with a method for adding in gentle ingredients to a dry mix and then pressing them so that they would keep their shape. The resulting 'bath bombs' were fizzy, fragrant and softened the water so that even those with sensitive skin would be able to bathe without irritation.

Champagne Bath

This bath bomb emulated a bottle of pink champagne once dropped into the water. With cognac essential oil alongside citrus and herbal notes, it was designed with decadence and celebration in mind. Wrapped in iridescent wrapping and tied with a pink ribbon, this was seen in all the best bathrooms.

The bath bombs started out fun and inventive and evolved (with the help of a crafty, design-savvy Rowena) into even more fun, shiny and delightful characters...

Blackberry Bath Bomb

This was the most popular of all the bath bombs. It came wrapped in shiny black paper with a long red fuse attached. In the bath it fizzed away in a cloud of blackberry fragrance. Its finishing flourish was a piece of paper that would surface and float to the top of the water bearing the legend BOOM BOOM!

Bombastic

With her provocative, pouting red lips, shiny lilac outfit and outrageous colourful strands of hair, Bombastic was a firm favourite. One customer comment featured in catalogue #11 requested '*Please keep Bombastic – just pulling it out of a parcel makes me laugh!*' Bombastic's name paid homage to the big beat and dance scene of the time and had an uplifting floral fragrance designed to get your body moving.

> '*I love your bathtime goodies so much, I want to share how good they are with all my friends – it seems such a waste to bathe alone.*'
> Sarah Gromett, Chichester, W. Sussex.

> Blackberry Bath Bomb – because it's scrummy and leaves your skin really soft.
> C Anderton – Leigh, Lancashire.

Damp Squid

This beguiling little fellow, recognisable for his googly eyes, was named after a customer complaint. When Jennifer of West Yorkshire wrote to say that something was a 'bit of a damp squid' (instead of damp squib) the team couldn't resist creating this frothy chap.

The Damp Squid was fragranced to be reminiscent of a gentle sea breeze, transporting the lucky bather to the ocean. A great attraction of this particular ballistic was that once he had finished fizzing you could throw him at your bathroom tiles and he would stick there!

In homage to the inspiration behind the idea, one of the first bath bombs was made in the shape of a tablet. These would appear in catalogues as a roll of Aqua Sizzlers so customers could create their own plink, fizz and bubble. Cosmetics to Go's second catalogue sagely advised,

'*Soothes the troubled brow, calms troubled skin. Perfect for bath-time thinkers and morning-after drinkers.*'

Customers loved the bath bombs. Throughout the life of Cosmetics to Go they would evolve into myriad different guises.

The Invention of the Bath Bomb | 43

Keeping Things Fresh
Constant innovation and evolution helped to keep things fresh!

Constantine & Weir and Dr Malcolm Stuart had set up a company called Albion Botanicals selling fresh cosmetics with a sell-by date. This company didn't last long.

A visit to a delicatessen in London re-inspired Rowena and Mark's enthusiasm for this fresh idea. In this particular deli you could choose which salad would go into your sandwich from a selection of silver bowls. Fresh chopped tomatoes, crisp cucumber, fragrant onions and myriad other choices were displayed for the customer.

Back in Poole, Susan Sievers set up in Mo's lab and began experimenting with ingredients. The face masks that were developed were full of fresh fruit and veggies and needed to be sent out the very same day they were made. These face masks were extremely effective, but had to be used quickly and kept in the refrigerator as the ingredients were all natural and no preservatives were used.

The face masks were bursting full of energetic, helpful enzymes to buff and brighten the skin. Some used oily fruit like avocadoes to moisturise and nourish, and others used asparagus for its calming, soothing properties. Cosmetics to Go were not only fruity experts, but also proud protestors

against the fashionable cosmetics movement that seemed to champion products based on newly discovered synthetic chemicals. They fought back using these fresh face masks as their cosmetic warriors.

How juicy can you go?! Face masks included whole fruits blended into the products to get the full goodness out. This is a tradition Lush have followed with their Fresh Face mask range and the tagline *'Yes! We really do put the whole fruit in!'*

A short story by the satirist Saki called 'Filboid Studge, The Story of the Mouse That Helped' inspired the name for this range. In it, a clever advertising man scared people into buying a particularly unappealing cereal called 'Filboid Studge' by illustrating a gloomy scene of unfortunate damned souls who had failed to buy any, trapped in hell and reaching out desperately with the caption 'They cannot buy it now!'. This simple campaign made the cereal a huge success, with everybody rushing to buy it.

So why did Cosmetics to Go adopt this name? Because they had the tricky task of encouraging people to put a yucky-looking goo onto their faces! The effects of the fresh face masks were amazing on the skin but didn't always look super appetising to apply... the name, and the face masks, stuck!

Carolyn mixes up a batch of face mask

This page was taken from Cosmetics to Go catalogue #11

Telephonists' guide to preservatives

Since the time our ancestors stopped making their beauty preparations in their own homes, preservatives have become a regular feature in cosmetics. For many items, creams, lotions, liquids, powders etc, it has been considered necessary to ensure a product lasts for a length of time. Micro-organisms and moulds that grow cannot always be seen. Legislation recommends a products shelf life should be a minimum of two years unless otherwise stated at the time of purchase. Most companies have opted to play it safe by putting large amounts of 'strong' preservatives into their products, unfortunately these materials are apt to cause irritations and problems on the skin.

It is also worth remembering that preservatives do not last forever. Each time a pot is opened or a dirty finger is dipped in, a little of the preservative is used up - it is not a renewable source - so keeping lids on and dirty fingers out will help prolong the life of any product.

WHOLE LEMON MASK
When we say whole lemon we mean the whole lemon is liquidised into this fresh citrus mask for its astringent and toning properties, mix this with the limeflower decoction, moisturising glycerin and finally deep cleansing kaolin and you have a refreshing, effective, mask for normal to oily skins.
For normal skins pH 3 Use within 6 weeks
All the ingredients in this product are (greatest first): Kaolin clay, Limeflower Decoction flowers boiled in water, Whole Lemon, Glycerin.

IT'LL BE WITH YOU IN THE SQUEEZING OF A LEMON.
OLIVER GOLDSMITH
She stoops to conquer

Belinda

Phil

STRAWBERRY AND GINGER BODY MASK
A powerful, stimulating mask for the body that works wonders on the upperarms, thighs and bottom and any other area (except the face) that looks a little sluggish, thanks to rubefacent strawberries and ginger that get the circulation flowing.
For sluggish skins pH 5.5 Use within 4 weeks
All the ingredients in this product are (greatest first): Glycerin, Kaolin, Strawberries, Papaya, Ginger Root, Ginger Essential Oil, Geranium Essential Oil.

KIWI SHAMPOO
Deep-cleansing Rhassoul Mud, fresh kiwi fruit and oranges in a mild shampoo base lathered into the hair and left for 5 - 10 minutes are just the thing for spring cleansing the scalp and greasy hair.
For Oily Hair and Problem Scals pH 6 Use within 4 weeks
All the ingredients in this product are (greatest first): Sodium Lauryl Sulphate shampoo base, Water, Oranges, Kiwi Fruit, Rhassoul Mud, Glycerin, Limeflowers, Sage, Geranium Essential Oil

WHEATGRASS MOISTURISER
A perfect example of plenty of glycerine to moisturise, helped along by a super limeflower decoction means that this wheatgrass, enzyme-rich shampoo lasts for a full six weeks. Add to this cocoa butter and almond oil for their superb skin smoothing properties and you've got a moisturiser to improve the skins condition not only on the face and neck but over the body too.
For all skins pH 7 Use within 6 weeks
All the ingredients in this product are (greatest first): Limeflower Decoction limeflowers boiled in water, Glycerin, Wheatgrass, Almond Oil, Stearic Acid vegetable emulsifying wax, Cocoa Butter, Ethyl Alcohol, Triethanolamine emulsifier, Carrageen seaweed extract to thicken, Geranium Essential Oil, Chamomile Essential Oil.

46 | COSMETICS TO GO

The work that Cosmetics to Go started by exploring preservative-free products continues at Lush, where product ranges are constantly reviewed to reduce preservative use wherever possible.

To Go's September Catalogue 1993

APPLE SMUDGE SHAMPOO

A pearly cream shampoo jam-packed with apples, cucumber, oatmeal, kaolin, glycerin and marigold petals to cleanse normal or chemically processed hair, leaving it soft, moisturised and manageable. Cleanses the scalp too, ridding it of any nasties - after all, a healthy scalp helps to keep the hair healthy too.

For Normal to Dry Hair   pH 6   Use within 4 weeks
All the ingredients in these products are (greatest first): Sodium Lauryl Sulphate shampoo base, Apples, Cucumber, Glycerin, Oatmeal, Kaolin, Limeflowers, Marigold Petals, Cinnamon Leaf Essential Oil, Tagettes Essential Oil

Penny

With these points in mind we choose to use 'low' irritancy preservatives, with a long history of being safe, (usually methylparaben, a water soluble preservative, and propylparaben an oil soluble preservative), and formulate carefully to ensure only the minimum amount is used where necessary, but these products will still have the recommended shelf life. Others within these pages have only the barest amount in, this means your product will last for the length of time that we recommend, Myddvai is an example of this. If we had included more preservative in this active mask many of you may have found it to cause irritation - as it is you won't.

Many other of our products contain no preservatives at all, soaps, bath bombs, Inasia shampoo bars are all examples of these.

The last group of products are those that contain no synthetic preservatives, are made fresh daily, should be kept in the fridge between uses and have a use by date on them. We use glycerine, a thick, clear, viscous liquid that is excellent for its moisturising properties and also helps to prevent micro organisms or moulds growing. In many of them there is also a decoction of lime flowers, and essential oils that have anti-microbial properties, thus helping to prolong their life. These are the Fridge products (and the three Really Cookin' hair varnishes).

Steve

PAPAYA CLEANSER

If your skin looks dull and sorry for itself this cleansing treatment will soon bring back a healthy glow. Used daily as part of your cleansing routine for the first week, and then alternative days, the enzyme papain in the papaya and the wheatgerm will slough away unwanted cells, dirt and grime to leave the skin looking really clean and glowingly healthy.

For all skins   pH 5   Use within 3 weeks
All the ingredients in this product are (greatest first): Glycerin, Kaolin, Papaya, Wheatgerm, Neroli Oil, Cinnamon Leaf Oil.

CUCUMBER CLEANSER

Cooling cucumber and clays deep cleanse, ground almonds very gently exfoliate and the fresh pineapples active enzyme digests dirt and grime to leave older skins looking young and fresh again.

For Thirty Something Skin   pH 6   Use within 3 weeks
All the ingredients in this product are (greatest first): Glycerin, Kaolin, Corn Starch, Limeflower Decoction limeflowers boiled in water, Ground Almonds, Fresh Cucumber, Fresh Pineapple, Olibanum Essential Oil, Geranium Essential Oil

GLORIOUS MUD PIE MASK

This one really is for wallowing in. Cover yourself in this squelchy brown mud mix and slip into a warm bath (not literally we hope!) and relax for about ten minutes, letting the body mask get to work. The glycerin keeps the product on the skin insulating it. Blood flows through the upper layers of the epidermis because of the warm water, sweating occurs and pores open allowing the rhassoul mud to deep cleanse and impurities to be released. Remove by massaging away, during which the brown rice flour gently exfoliates unwanted dead skin cells.

pH 6   Use within 4 weeks
All the ingredients in this product are (greatest first): Glycerin, Water, Kaolin, Brown Rice Flour, Rhassoul Mud, Limeflowers, Star Anise, Lavender Essential Oil, Litsea Cubeba Essential Oil, Cinnamon Leaf Essential Oil.

When the Filboid Studge range was first introduced it was called Keep In The Fridge.

Keeping Things Fresh | 47

Hop Along to the Herb King

In 1981, Alan Hopking qualified as a herbalist and was looking for a clinic from where to ply his new trade. He saw there was a room available at 29 High Street, popped along to meet everybody and discovered that they had many shared interests. Mark, of course, was particularly interested in using herbal treatments and remedies for his trichology patients, and Alan, having just completed his training, was a great partner to enthuse with. It was agreed that he would take the available room as a base for his herbal clinic.

Each morning he would make his way into work from a caravan that he shared with his wife on a small plot of land. When Mark found out the living arrangements he declared, 'Well, you need a house!' They worked it out together with solicitors and estate agents and managed to get him into a house and onto the property ladder.

Although Alan was to eventually move his clinic out of 29 High Street and into his own premises in Christchurch, he and Mark stayed in touch. They continued to discuss the effects of various tinctures and herbal ingredients on the hair and skin and kept each other up to date on what they were learning about or developing.

Alan Hopking

Mark had written the book *Herbal Hair Colouring* in 1978, which explored the history of hair dyeing, explained the chemistry of modern hair and revealed the natural colouring properties of herbs. The book also featured some of Mark's recipes, including his expert recommendations for blending henna with other ingredients to achieve the perfect shades for his customers' hair. In Lush, these recipes were developed further and are sold as henna bricks.

In 2022, Lush writer Milly Ahlquist and Mark Constantine undertook an extensive rewrite of his book, and published it as *True Colours: Hair Colouring for the Curious and the Cautious*. Henna has been used as a hair and skin dye for thousands of years, holding deep cultural significance in traditions and rituals across the Middle East, Asia and Africa, and the book explores these as well as the history and science of hair dye. The book was printed using a unique henna ink blend created especially for it in a collaboration between Lush, local printer Dayfold, and ink manufacturer PMS.

Alan sorts out the henna

Alan sorts out the henna. Alan took charge of sourcing the henna for Mark's hair care and colour formulations.

'We were interested in fresh and natural ingredients, yet every other salesman was knocking at our door, trying to sell us the latest new miracle beauty chemical or some kind of nasty concoction, then I got a call from Alan. He was a lovely bloke trying to flog me fresh herbs. It was a breath of fresh air. I thought I'd have some of that!'
Mark Constantine

Mark found himself uninspired by the salespeople who would constantly cold call trying to sell ingredients for their products. These callers did not understand the premise of using natural ingredients and were only offering new chemical formulations or unappealing synthetics.

A well-timed phone call from Alan, however, informing the company that he had moved into supplying plants and herbs, sparked an idea. Not only did the company decide to buy from him but they also asked him to research and write reports on natural ingredients that they used or wanted to know more about.

These reports outlined the properties and benefits of plants such as nettles, camomile and seaweed when used in cosmetics. These were then passed to the Cosmetics to Go press team. They would send them to beauty magazines and scientific journals providing publicity for natural ingredients and reminding the public of the qualities to be found in the fresh fruits, vegetables and plants all around them.

Alan's research on lesser-known plants and herbs also opened up exciting avenues for the team, who got to work with new materials that they had never used before. The team were keen to keep learning and built up a database of botanical information that would prove invaluable.

Mark and Alan were also to work together experimenting on what natural ingredients would successfully act as hair dyes. Having mastered the henna colours they were eager to see how they could expand the range. The challenge was finding a naturally occurring ingredient that would remain in the hair and survive washings. During periods of research the corridors of the factories and offices were brightened up with Cosmetics to Go staff testing the latest beetroot pink or carrot orange!

Botanomancy

Geoffrey Grigson wrote over seventy books in his lifetime on subjects ranging from botany and poetry to art and the countryside. The inspiration for the Botanomancy range came from his botanical books, in particular, *A Herbal of Sorts*.

Myddvai would evolve to become Mask of Magnaminty and appears in the Lush skin care range.

The Cosmetics to Go team were a literate bunch. Wordiness reigned supreme, especially when it came to deciding the names for the eclectically monikered delights of the Botanomancy range…

Written as an ode to the Plant Age, when plants were all-important in day-to-day life, it is full of interesting anecdotes and stories about all things flora. You might recognise a few familiar words in there, appropriated by the creative team for product names.

The word Botanomancy came from this book. It describes the art of using plants as a fortune-telling method. Whether you play *'he loves me, he loves me not'* with flower petals or burn aromatic branches to interpret the meanings of the fire and smoke – botanomancy is what you're doing!

The word was deemed perfect for this new herbal range as Botanomancy featured a range of lotions and potions including ingredients from myriad flowers, plants and herbs.

Amaranthine cleansing lotion was named after the mythical plant Amaranthus, whose flower was eternally in bloom and never faded. An apt sentiment to remember as you gently wiped away the day's dirt with this milky cleanser.

A herb walk led by Alan Hopking inspired the invention of Quishion, a super-moisturising hand cream. Its name was a blend of the words, quince and cushion, because it included quince seed mucilage and because it was so rich and soothing it was like a cushion for your hands.

Ianthine means 'violet' and was named after the colour of the lavender flowers used in this body lotion. Alan Hopking was a huge fan of lavender. In his report on its properties, he bemoaned its popularity. A victim of its own success as the many beneficial properties it boasted were overlooked by its ubiquity.

Smaragadine was named after its rich, emerald-green colour. This popular bath and shower gel smelled of earthy patchouli and sweet geranium and could convince you that you were bathing in a forest if you closed your eyes and breathed deeply. Herbal ingredients included nettles and peppermint alongside rose and orange peel. This was also a precursor to the Tramp shower gel found in Lush's Retro range.

Each product had its own magical, evocative name to match.

Myddvai was the name of the clay-rich, exfoliating face and back pack. This was one of the customer's favourite products for its powerful spot-banishing effects. To all those waking up the next day to blemish-free skin it must have seemed like a magical poultice.

It was named after the fabled Physicians of Myddfai. This legendary family of doctors from Carmarthenshire used herbs and plants to make remedies to cure the sick. Their reputation for herb lore grew until they were renowned throughout mediaeval Europe.

Myths about their magical powers grew, and it was rumoured that they had inherited supernatural healing powers from the fairy of the lake Llyn-y-Fan.

It was said that once tempted from the lake, the fairy and their father had fallen in love, married and had the three boys. The story ends sadly, as after striking his wife three times, she fled back to the lake, leaving the sons behind.

Before the fairy left the mortal realm, she appeared to her three boys and told them it was their fate to relieve the pain and suffering of mankind. She showed them a place called Pant y Meddygon (Physicians Dingle), where healing plants grew, and taught them the magical art of healing. These abandoned sons were to become the Physicians of Myddfai and unlocked the medicinal secrets of herbs and flowers.

Whizz forward some centuries to Poole Harbour, where the botanical magicians of the nineties, the Cosmetics to Go team, resided and used all their skills and resources to follow the work the legendary Physicians started.

Alan Hopking's specially commissioned botanic research was used alongside ancient herbal recipes and methods. They also dabbled in some modern alchemy using a hot shot of steam through ingredients to emulsify them quickly. This resulted in beautifully absorbent blends that sank straight into the skin and the 'steam creams' that resulted featured in this range.

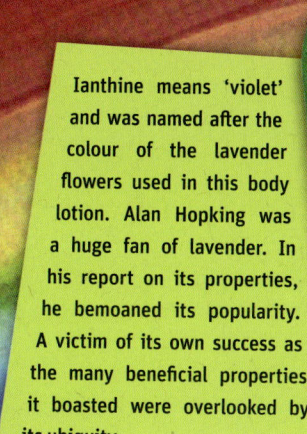

Please don't discontinue the Botanomancy range - They are utterly essential to my well being and peace of mind.
F Robertson - Birchington, Kent.

The Botanomancy pages were always exciting to turn to, as the bottles appeared like magical green gems nestled against a leafy or fairy-influenced backdrop. Within the crazy colourfulness of a Cosmetics to Go catalogue, the Botanomancy pages were always calm, enchanting and welcomed flower fairies of all descriptions.

You Spin Me Right Round

The inspiration, thought and attention that went into products was reflected when it came to packaging and labels. Beautiful and enchanting ingredients on the inside, and unique packaging with a Cosmetics to Go twist on the outside...

Each of the labels printed on these products featured an optical illusion, so spinning the lid or the bottle would produce magical effects. Butterflies would appear to fly into the air, mesmerising circles would draw you in and yellow men would run around and around in circles.

The lengthy names included such gems as Cosmetics to Go's Unusually Thick & Thin, Rich But Not Greasy At All Hand & Body Moisturiser. These were a homage to fellow cosmetics firm Kiehl's, whose products all featured verbose names. In 1990, Kiehl's was still an independent company known for its traditional drugstore look, and the team had visited its quirky shop on a trip to New York and had been inspired. Later it would be bought by L'Oréal.

Cosmetics to Go was the first company to develop labels that peeled back so they could add more information underneath. This extra space came in handy, as they were also one of the first UK companies to produce a quantitative ingredients list (Q.I. for short) on their product labels. This detailed every single ingredient used so the customer could see exactly what they were getting.

Because of the numerous ranges that Cosmetics to Go created, the costs for all the different labels that had to be designed and printed were considerable. Extraordinary and exclusive packaging for products kept the unique look of the brand and allowed for creativity, but it also had a downside.

Mo remembers finding cupboards and shelves full of unused labels because product lines could sometimes be discontinued after just a couple of issues of the catalogue and then they were useless. Not only that, but the ordering of new stock was somewhat chaotic, as was storage and inventory. Often duplicates were ordered without people realising there were already thousands of those exact labels in a dark corner somewhere.

'*So this is where all the money is,*' she observed wryly.

This smiley bottle of **Cosmetic to Go's Oh Go On, Lazy Sunday Afternoon Nutty Massage Oil** contained coconut, almond, sesame and orchid oil for a moisturising massage.

This was snappily named **Cosmetic to Go's Non Sticky, Non Smelly, Non Blocking, Non Aerosol, No Nonsense Deodorant** – imagine asking to borrow that in the gym!

Cosmetics to Go's Unusually Thick & Thin, Rich But Not Greasy At All Hand and Body Moisturiser was thicker in winter and thin in the summer. The loose emulsion allowed the water-based ingredients to sink in to moisturise and the oily, buttery ingredients to stay on the skin and soften.

This hypnotic black pot held **Cosmetics to Go's Luxurious, Not Too Light, Just Right, No Longer Tight, Dry Face Moisturiser,** a facial cream containing orchid oil, almond oil and wheatgerm oil.

You Spin Me Right Round | 53

CHS... The Catalogue Vision

Design was incredibly important to Cosmetics to Go, especially when it came to their iconic range of catalogues.

In 1988, the team asked Clive Holmes Studios (CHS), a graphic design house based in Christchurch, Dorset, to work on their cosmetics catalogue. After the first meeting they realised it was going to be extremely tricky to please this new client! Mark had strong ideas and was determined to develop a catalogue that would really stand out from everything else. It was a steep learning curve regarding all aspects of his approach.

Among the list of requirements, it had to portray an 'off the wall' feel and all the products were to be shown using painstakingly airbrushed images and not photographs. The writing style needed to be expressive and descriptive with quirky copy and headlines. They also wanted to include contributions from the readers in as many product stories as possible. The catalogues also needed to be completely ethical, emphasise that no products were tested on animals and recycled materials needed to be used in the printing. (They could see the team 'walking the walk', as it were, when they realised that Mark did not drive and would only travel to meetings in staff vehicles which had to run on diesel.)

Creatively, this was a great challenge, and CHS relied heavily on their experience as designers and a vast collection of magazines and publications that they could use in coming up with creative solutions to realise the team's concepts.

Unlike today in the age of the internet, people were not able to just google for information for the articles. Anything written had to be researched through interviews or investigations, or going to libraries and researching articles. Proper journalistic and time-consuming endeavours were the order of the day.

The writers had a tough time of it too! Marcia Harrison and Chris Flynn, who were responsible for lots of the catalogue copy along with Rowena and others, remember Mark coming in with a poem one morning, and saying *'See what you can do with this.'* No context, just handed over the poem and wandered off.

The late and much-loved Clive Holmes pitches a spread

The meeting room window at CHS which Mark climbed out of, narrowly missing the rose bush!

54 | Cosmetics to Go

Different product ranges lent themselves to different artistic styles. Here the kitsch S.W.A.L.K. range goes pop art.

Each catalogue meeting was generally full of tension and ideas and sometimes disagreements. At one of the usual difficult and frustrating catalogue meetings when no one could agree the way forward with a new product launch, Mark suddenly stood up, opened the sash window and climbed out, narrowly missing a prickly rose bush outside! He was last seen disappearing off down the road. He was either bored with how the meeting was going or he had spotted a particularly rare species of bird.

'Where is Mark off to?!'

Mark was a huge birdwatching enthusiast and on several occasions he would get a call, stop the meeting and vanish on a trip across Dorset to see a rare bird. This actually led to CHS hand-making twenty or so prototype bird-watching games called *Twitch*. These were the kind of random diversions that sprang from creative catalogue meetings.

Looking for inspiration

Blue sky thinking?

CHS... The Catalogue Vision | 55

Photographs, airbrushed product illustrations and traditional drawings would all sit together to create unique page layouts.

During these meetings it was important to be aware of doing anything silly or daft, like climbing onto a desk to look at a photograph more closely, or modeling a new crazy style of shower cap. More than likely someone would ambush you with a camera and next thing you knew you were in print on the pages of the next catalogue.

The catalogue was originally produced two or three times a year. However, it turned out to be so popular with a real cult following that it was decided to start sending catalogues out on a monthly basis.

Beware! Steve Pierson at work!

Every single catalogue took a huge amount of effort and resources. With no computers, mock-up pages were more like collages, with all manner of magazine imagery, photocopies and photos cut out then stuck together to create a look for a spread. Talk about real-life cut and paste! Headings were hand-drawn or Letraset lettering applied and parallel lines drawn to indicate where copy was to go.

Each spread would consist of a baseboard, which had all the background images of the original photos or illustrations stuck in place. Then the various other images were on separate overlays and on top of that the type layer was attached. Finally, a tracing paper sheet was put over the top onto which all the instructions to the printers would be written. And this was for each individual spread!

Mark's insistence that all product images were illustrated also created additional challenges. Originally inspired by Pat Ziegler's illustrations in the Banana Republic catalogues that the team adored, it meant that all artwork requests needed to be sent to airbrush illustrators in London and there seemed to always be a time delay waiting for the artists to complete the work.

Another hazard in those days was making type or copy amendments to the artwork. Everything had to be done painstakingly on the drawing board with scalpels and parallel rulers to reposition type. The designers joked that you could almost always guarantee a single letter you had cut out would fly off and you'd lose it. You'd search frantically for it or hope that on another bit of unused typeset copy you had a spare letter, only to discover it stuck to your elbow in the evening when you got home!

The challenges of each catalogue pushed the designers and writers to come up with extraordinary and unexpected solutions and prose. Rowena remembers describing each soap in the range as if it was a radio programme with its own personality and style. Marcia remembers being sent off to interview two elderly ladies who owned an antique shop and adored the Ginger perfume. It was this eccentric and bohemian approach that produced such rich, original and unexpected catalogues.

All the ingredients contained in this designer are (greatest first): Humour *essential oil when dealing with Cosmetics To Go,* Caffeine *coffee grains steeped in boiling water,* Mischief, Self-Control, Plain Chocolate Biscuits *soothing and calming.*

How to use: Agitate to breaking point, apply to slightly warmed seat and relax for 4 to 5 days. (Shakes well during use). The catalogue should be left smooth and fresh (ha! ha!) - use at least once a week.

This image of Clive Holmes was taken from Catalogue #9

Traditional British comic books inspired all the Cosmetics to Go Christmas catalogues.

The catalogue spreads shown here were picked especially by CHS staff who used to work on Cosmetics to Go catalogues and have been designing this book alongside us!

CHS... The Catalogue Vision | 57

Cosmetics to Go used their catalogues to share their values with customers. They were dedicated to campaigning against animal testing in cosmetics. This page was taken from Cosmetics to Go catalogue #8.

CToG's POLICY ON

One thing which nags me a little is as I missed the actual launching of CTG I wonder exactly what your policies on animal testing, ingredients in products etc are? Y. Barnett - Cambridge.

CRUELTY FREE - THE FINAL PHASE
AN OPEN LETTER FROM COSMETICS TO GO

At COSMETICS TO GO, our prime concern is the customer. So when it comes to ensuring product safety we choose the methods we know to be the most effective - and the most humane. And those methods do not involve animals - for the simple reason that animal tests do not reliably predict the *human* response to a product or ingredient, as reports have shown. In short - animal tests are expensive, inaccurate and inhumane.

Recently, due both to consumer pressure and to beauty companies like ourselves making and selling cruelty-free cosmetics, many of the multinational cosmetics giants have been forced to change their policies and adopt alternative, non-animal testing methods.

However - how many people realise that 60% of animal testing is in fact carried out by raw material suppliers?

A few years ago, in order to put pressure on these raw material suppliers, some companies agreed on a moratorium, stating that they would not buy a material animal tested after 1976, the date of the last EC Cosmetics Directive.

In 1980, however, along with the BUAV, COSMETICS TO GO developed the concept of the five year rule - ie, we refused to buy any ingredient or material from a supplier which had been tested on animals within the previous five years. This both discouraged retrospective testing, and gave other cosmetic companies the chance to join our crusade by working towards their own cruelty-free criteria within a reasonable and realistic time span.

Yet despite these and other efforts, suppliers continue to use animals in their safety tests. And - what is worse - by selling us non-animal tested, standard materials (such as Bicarbonate of Soda and Citric Acid) these suppliers make a profit - which is then reinvested in the animal testing of new raw materials.

In other words - our money is indirectly and inadvertently subsidising the testing of raw materials on animals.

SO - WHERE TO NOW . . . ?

We at COSMETICS TO GO have decided that it is time to take our cruelty-free stance to its logical conclusion with a new, more positive and radical policy. Put simply - from now on we intend asking of all our suppliers what our customers ask of us.

We will not buy from - and therefore invest money in - any companies which test *any* of their raw materials on animals, or even if *their* suppliers test on animals - whether we buy that material or not.

COSMETICS TO GO customers look for a corporate anti-vivisection stance on all of our products - we, as customers, are now demanding the same of our suppliers. When we say we do not support animal testing - we mean it. Our aim is an honest, cradle to grave cruelty-free policy, right across the board.

Over the last few months, this new stand has led to a great flurry of activity in Poole. No stone has been left unturned in the worldwide search for alternative, totally cruelty-free companies to supply the ingredients for our ranges. Products have had to be re-formulated and ingredients re-sourced to ensure that COSMETICS TO GO customers would not lose out due to the new demands we are making of our suppliers.

Yet we are not asking the impossible of these suppliers - there *are* perfectly viable alternatives to animal tests for ensuring product safety. In 1979, the European Parliament recommended that the EC, should 'formulate a draft framework directive with the aim of ending the use of animals for decorative cosmetic testing'. Yet there was no co-ordinated, scientifically sound study of

The volunteer pictured here is Chris Flynn, one of the writers that worked on the catalogues. Cosmetics to Go staff would get involved and took part in the human test trials.

C.T.G. people breathe in powders and then take lung function tests to see the effects.

WE WILL NOT BUY FROM COMPANIES

Cosmetics to Go

THE TESTING OF RAW MATERIALS

viable alternatives available to the EC for reference - so in 1990 COSMETICS TO GO commissioned a worldwide survey of alternative testing techniques from Dr Gill Langley of the Hadwen Trust. We then presented this report to the EC as just that reference.

To truly influence the EC, however, we need the support of our raw material suppliers - after all, they are the ones carrying out the animal tests - so we sent the report to each and every one of them too. The report shows, in black and white, what we have long believed - that non-animal tests make sense economically, morally and in terms of ensuring standards of safety. The alternatives are there. The safety standards are there. The market is there. Suppliers can no longer hide behind any of these arguments while they continue to use animals in their safety tests.

Commissioning the report was only the beginning - these tests have to be *used* - suppliers must authorize alternative tests, we cannot do it for them. And COSMETICS TO GO is going to use all of its influence to force suppliers to adopt these safe alternatives.

In a few years consumer power has moved the EC closer to a non-animal testing policy for the beauty industry. With the weight of consumer power and of sympathetic suppliers behind us we feel that the long battle against vivisection in cosmetics could be nearing its close. We sincerely hope that we will be joined in our new policy by other companies with a conscience - this could then be the final and conclusive battle in the campaign.

We ask for your support.

News from BUAV
British Union for the Abolition of Vivisection, 16a Crane Grove, London N7 8LB.
Telephone 071-607 9533. Fax 071- 700 0252.
campaigning to end animal experiments

PRESS STATEMENT ON COSMETICS TO GO'S NEW 'CRUELTY-FREE' CRITERIA

Cosmetics To Go's new 'non-animal' testing criteria is yet another positive initiative from a company that makes a habit of them. Rather than remain satisfied with the standard 5 year or fixed date criteria adopted by other 'cruelty-free' firms, they have carefully thought out a new way of guaranteeing to their customers that they do their utmost to avoid any involvement in animal testing. The BUAV welcomes any such move which is aimed at putting pressure on the many suppliers of cosmetic raw materials who continue to support crude, cruel animal tests.

There can be no doubt that Cosmetics To Go's new criteria will do just that. We will be interested to watch how raw material suppliers react to being blacklisted for their animal tests by a leading 'cruelty-free' manufacturer. We are therefore pleased to offer Cosmetics To Go our endorsement of their initiative and to welcome the opportunity to continue the close working relationship we have had with them in recent years.

Steve McIvor
BUAV Campaigns Director
5th June 1991

Dr Ozone Hairspray
One ingredient we haven't been able to re-source is Butyl Ester of PVM/MA Copolymer. We've got stock at present to make enough bottles to last until next January (1992).

Dr Ozone's Stranglehold Hairspray
All the ingredients contained in this product are (greatest first): Ethyl Alcohol, Butyl Ester of PVM/MA Copolymer gum to hold hair stiff, Triethanolamine emulsifier, Fragrance, Dimethicone Copolyol silicone to coat and protect the hair, Coconut oil, Sandalwood Essential Oil, Lemon Essential Oil, Palmarosa Essential Oil, Galbanum, Bergamot Essential Oil.

ALTERNATIVES TO ANIMAL TESTS IN COSMETIC TOXICOLOGY

A REVIEW OF DEVELOPMENT AND VALIDATION

A technical submission for consideration by the European Commission

Commissioned by Constantine & Weir Plc
By Gill Langley MA PhD MIBiol

This report is available from Constantine & Weir Plc, 29 High Street, Poole, Dorset, BH15 1AB, United Kingdom

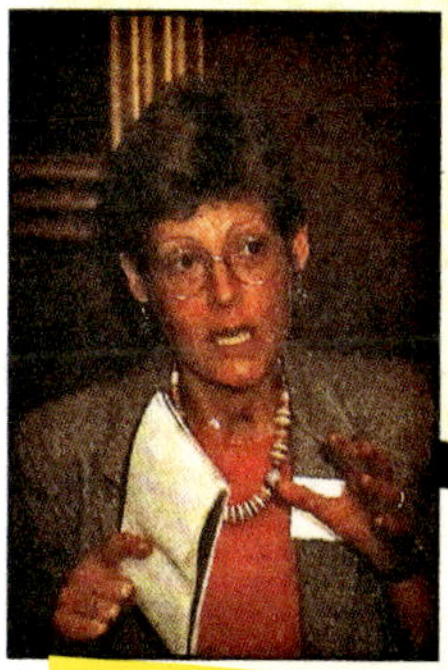

Steve McIvor (above) and Gill Langley (left), guest speakers at the press launch of our new "cruelty-free" criteria on June 20th 1991.

If Cosmetics to Go could not find ingredients that followed their strict no testing on animals policy they would look for alternative ingredients and change the product formula. (Sometimes having to discontinue the product while the reformulation was taking place in the labs.)

WHO TEST ON ANIMALS!!!

Fighting Animal Testing | 59

The Assisi Project

Liz had been researching alternative cruelty-free options for testing cosmetics and had flown to America to meet research scientists as well as talk with the Fund for the Replacement of Animals in Medical Experiments in the UK.

Frustrated at the lack of cruelty-free safety tests, they decided to commission a project to develop one themselves. Helen had been working on a range for babies with her young sons in mind and wanted to ensure this would be safe and tested.

Liz and Helen talked to local consultant Neil Butler, who was an expert in his field on microorganisms, and Jill Langley from the Dr Hadwen Trust, the UK's leading non-animal medical research charity, to help.

The test they most wanted to replace was the particularly cruel Draize test. This involved dripping ingredients into the eyes of rabbits to measure irritancy. They began to develop what would become The Assisi Test. The company invested thousands of pounds into this project. It was an issue that was close to the hearts of staff and customers alike, who all cared deeply about putting a stop to testing on animals and using non-animal-based alternatives.

The test was revolutionary. The cultures tested were held within serums based on milk and yeast and not animal-based serums – a first of its kind and a breakthrough. The Assisi Test was announced to the press at the famous Ivy restaurant in London.

Cosmetics to Go also teamed up with the British Union for the Abolition of Vivisection (BUAV). This campaigning charity was dedicated to eliminating testing on animals and the partnership helped publicise the test and tried to encourage other companies to use the research.

Cosmetics to Go would not buy ingredients from a supplier who tested any of their raw materials on animals. This policy* was something the company was dedicated to and very proud of. It was also announced at the press conference at the Ivy restaurant.

This strict guiding principle is upheld today in Lush, where they are still fighting animal testing. On the anniversary of the Assisi Test announcement, in 2012, Mark returned to the Ivy to hold a press conference where he announced a £250,000 annual prize fund to promote anti-cruelty testing research. As he sums up so adroitly, '*We've been fighting all this time and I really would like to see an end to this in my lifetime.*'

* You can check this policy out on pages 58–59

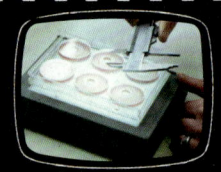

Tested on Humans

Cosmetics to Go often needed willing volunteers who would help to test out their brand-new inventions. They had their own test centre on the premises at 29 High Street and would often invite people in to come and try out products in development.

You might be lucky and take part in a trial enjoying a hands-on massage, or a free beauty treatment. Some of the tests were a little more vigorous. Karl Bygrave, now a Lush Director but then a long-standing member of staff from the Constantine & Weir days, recalls relaxing in front of UV lamps in the name of sunscreen testing!

New hair inventions were also tested onsite in the hair salon that existed in 29 High Street. Willing volunteers were found and then the latest shampoos, conditioners, treatments and colours would be put to the test.

We've found some hair test forms showing different treatments tested on some familiar faces...

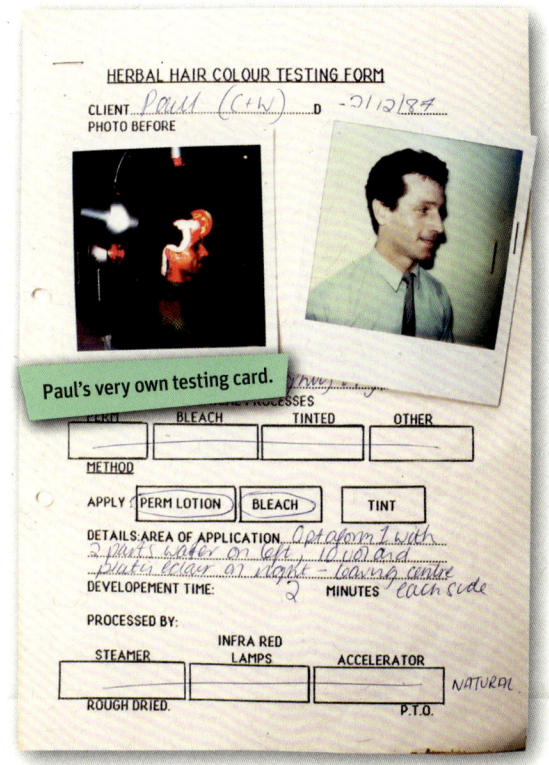

Paul's very own testing card.

Paul

Paul Greeves, chemist by trade and qualification, came to Cosmetics to Go to manage the labs. He was involved in various testing procedures and ran the research on sunscreens. Later he would move into the IT side of the business.

Liz tests a foot treatment. It's a tough job but someone's got to do it...

The Assisi Project & Tested on Humans | 61

Baby

Leap Year Babies! On Cosmetics to Go's 1st birthday, 29 February 1989, they advertised for any Leap Year babies who shared this special anniversary with them and those whose parents wrote in received a free Baby Revels Knapsack to make up for the disappointment of their children not getting a 'proper' birthday until 1992.

Cosmetics to Go was a child-friendly business. Lots of young parents worked at the company and pictures of their children decorated the various office desks and factory walls.

Helen Ambrosen also had two little boys and when her second, Robin, came along she decided she wanted safe, cruelty-free baby products for her children. This was a big impetus for all her work on the Assisi project.

Helen and Rowena visited daycare centres and nurseries to talk to new mothers to learn what they wanted from their baby care products. Taking their comments on board, and using her knowledge of natural ingredients, Helen developed a range full of essentials for the newest little humans.

The ingredients she chose were naturally gentle and effective. Marigold and camomile were picked to provide a comforting fragrance as well as for the soothing and calming properties of their essential oils.

Baby Revels babies were the proud owners of creams for their bottom, oils for their scalp and body, soothing lotion, dusting powder, sunscreen for those sunny days in the buggy, shampoo and even

Baby Revels research at the crèche

Revels

their own tooth gel. What more could the discerning infant desire?

Rowena also lent her inventive packaging skills and designed a baby bag made of nappy towelling fabric. It was the perfect size to pop the entire Baby Revels range into, and when it was folded and tucked properly it looked just like a baby's bottom in a nappy.

Many parents remember this range with a fond nostalgia as it reminds them of their little one's formative years. Helen wanted it to have a beautiful and distinctive smell that would remind parents of a special time that they shared with their children. It looks as if she achieved her wish!

Not only this, but pictures of the babies of both staff and customers were used in the pages of the catalogues. After all, who could resist sharing all the cute baby pictures that were sent in?

Customers sent in pictures of their beautiful babies.

Explorer Ranulph Fiennes

BELOW ZERO

The snowfall was quickening, leaving deep drifts of soft snow which made dragging the heavy sleds behind them a much harder task. Ranulph Fiennes and his team were being slowed down and provisions were running low.

Temperatures never rose above -10°C and on the coldest nights were dropping to -57°C. When the winds picked up it was as though the freezing air buffeting them came from the icy gates of hell itself...

Ranulph slipped out his Frostbite lip protector and grimly applied it to lips blue with cold. As the smell of the moisturising balm made his stomach rumble with hunger he thought,

> *'I wonder if this would be good to eat?!'*

When the Below Zero range was being developed little did the inventors know that it would eventually find its way to the icy wastes of the Arctic...

Helen had met a researcher who was studying the effects of the cold on skin as part of a research project for the Royal Air Force. He was looking at the physical effects on pilots if the windscreen of their jet was smashed in the air. Specifically, he was exploring what the effects of a sudden plummet in temperature would have on their ability to keep flying.

He and Helen shared theories with each other on ingredients that would protect the skin. The researcher had found that it was important to use ingredients that would warm the skin up, so this prompted her to experiment with materials like ginger and peppermint that would stimulate blood flow to the extremities. The whole philosophy for the Below Zero range was based around these observations.

Helen went about amassing a range fit for an Arctic exploration, as it came to light that the finished products would be used by none other than esteemed explorer Ranulph Fiennes on a quest to reach the North Pole.

His team took these prototype products with them on their epic expedition and tested them in the field. After a gruelling time in deep, heavy snowfall that prevented them from being able to carry enough supplies to last, they were forced to turn back before reaching their destination. Despite not reaching the tip of the world, they had used the Below Zero range in the ghastly conditions and reported back to Cosmetics to Go with their thoughts and suggestions for improvements on the performance of the range.

> The Polar Bandit wristband held Alacalufa skin protector, Blockski sunblock and Frostbite lip-saver and each were marked in a traffic light colour of red, amber and green for ease of use on the go.

Below Zero | 65

Companions

Sending the intrepid team out to have an epic Africa Companion adventure was just part of an even more revolutionary and crazy idea of Jeff Osment. Mark came up with the idea of a video catalogue. His old best pal from school, Jeff, was now an experienced director producing commercials and videos, so it came to pass that Mark asked Jeff to get involved.

Jeff said: 'While I was looking through various books, I saw this picture of an African elephant in a game park with Mount Kilimanjaro behind it with its snowy peaks. I thought we could journey from the plains all the way up to the top of Kilimanjaro testing the cosmetics on the way...'

Jeff's original idea was to call the video 'Cosmetics to Go on Holiday' and show customers using the products in different locations. The Cosmetics to Go press team were keen on the idea. However, they suggested rather than using customers, Susannah Kenton, an up-and-coming journalist and presenter, should front the piece instead. Rowena was happy to be the co-presenter as she was eager to visit Tanzania and loved the idea of her first far-flung adventure. In the end, as you have seen on page 13, the trip became much more than anything Rowena could have imagined and turned into a struggle for survival.

Straight after arriving back home, with the film in the can and feeling a little worse for wear, Jeff began coordinating more filming.

A trip to Galway in Ireland was planned where they would interview a seaweed farmer who provided carrageen seaweed for the Sea Level range. This was an opportunity to show natural ingredients being gathered. This time Mark would be the interviewer and present the footage.

Unfortunately for the team, they were to arrive in Galway Bay at the same time as a huge Atlantic storm. Seafaring conditions became extremely dangerous, with waves so high that it became too dangerous to film on the boat. Back on land, the cameras gave up the ghost in the relentless rain and stopped working in the damp conditions. Reluctantly, they were forced to cancel the shoot. What a waste!

When everyone returned to Poole, they were despondent at the failure to complete the video, but very glad to have survived the scary sea conditions. Jeff took Mark to one side and said: 'Look Mark, we can't keep doing this. We've got the film in the can, but the rest of these assignments are going to kill us! Let's go ahead and put this out as The African Companions video. Let's just get it out there.'

Mark agreed. It took clever editing to replace some footage that had been lost but a short film was made and eventually appeared on the pages of the catalogue as The African Companions video.

The rest of the video catalogue sadly never materialised. It was these kind of prescient ideas that prompted Karl to explain that *'Cosmetics to Go was an internet company that arrived before the internet was invented.'* The company was so ahead of the time that the technology was just not in place to help them achieve their wild ambitions.

Jeff's skills were again called upon when he was asked to provide a multi-sensory experience for visitors to the Cosmetics to Go factory. He and Jeff Brown devised what would be named 'Smellyvision' and was a real treat for the senses.

Sparing no expense, a short film was made all about the essential rose oils used in many of the products. Filming took place in Morocco in the foothills of the Atlas Mountains during the rose harvest season. In the factory during these viewings they had devised a way of releasing rose fragrance into the air, so the audience were aromatically transported to the sunny fields they were viewing.

At the end of the showing, each audience member was also given Turkish Delight to eat, so the taste buds were involved in the experience too.

Jeff Osment

Jeff

Jeff met Mark at cub scouts and by the time they left grammar school at sixteen, they were best friends. While Mark trained as a hairdresser in Weymouth, Jeff studied film production at Bournemouth College of Art. Three years later they moved to London to find their fortune and shared a bedsit in Kensington, living off a diet of porridge and fish fingers.

Jeff went on to become an award-winning film producer and travelled the world making commercial films and videos, including African Companions and Smellyvision for his friend who now owned Cosmetics to Go. He was the producer of LUSH TV for many years.

Smellyvision stimulated all senses...

Forces Favourites

Luckily for everyone concerned, Rowena never did get around to handing in her notice after her misadventures up the mountain and returned safely to Poole. Once back in the labs and not travelling the world in the name of cosmetic research, she could be found indulging her childhood passion and creating colourful make-up ranges.

The Cosmetics to Go team loved looking back through history and being inspired by the past. While the fashion tide was awash with light blue eye shadow and bright pink cheeks, the creative team were busy developing a quietly sophisticated, retro make-up range to be called Forces Favourites.

Inspired by the women who 'mended and made-do' during the war efforts, and charmed by the look of this period, they decided to follow the make-up trends of those times. Tins, glass bottles and jars were used to package the range and old-fashioned ingredients such as rosewater, beeswax and glycerine made an appearance in the form of Cold Cream cleanser and Vanishing Cream moisturiser.

One of the wartime make-up rituals that grabbed the attention of the team was how resourceful women managed in the absence of stockings. Stockings were incredibly hard to get hold of during rationing but women still wanted to look their best. The trick was to cover their legs with gravy and then ask a friend to draw a line with a pencil all the way up the back of their legs. This would create the illusion of a pair of stocking-clad pins.

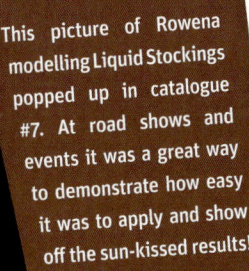

This picture of Rowena modelling Liquid Stockings popped up in catalogue #7. At road shows and events it was a great way to demonstrate how easy it was to apply and show off the sun-kissed results!

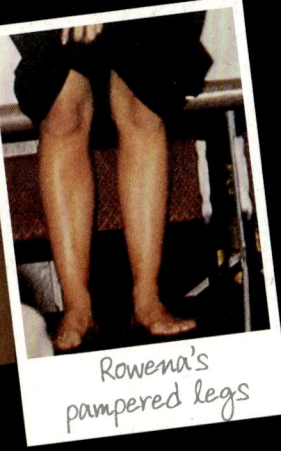

Rowena's pampered legs

Fast-forward to Cosmetics to Go's Liquid Stockings, which when smoothed onto pasty legs resulted in a bronzed glow, making them look just lovely.

The Mistress's Lipstick was a vibrant scarlet lip stain that lasted for ages. There were giggles during development stages as Stan and Rowena spent a lot of time stained red during testing. The base was plaster of Paris mixed with a rich crimson pigment, hence the fabulously long-lasting properties.

The lipsticks came wrapped in red foil with a piece of sandpaper enclosed, which you would use to sharpen the pencil. You would then dip the stick into the water, and apply it to your lips where it would set, leaving you perfectly kissable all night long.

This range also saw the introduction of the Cosmetics to Go Ration Book. This was a booklet of coupons that customers could buy and use against future purchases. This book was full of freebies and deals, which was perfect for fans of the brand.

The customer paid £5 to receive the book, and inside would find bundles of discounts, free items and special offers containing around £40 worth of savings. This was a nifty idea designed to get customers interested in products that they might not normally try and also to keep them coming back for their staples at reduced prices. It was all about building up customer numbers and repeat business, and it looked just the part too. Issued by a fictional Ministry of Cosmetics, it came complete with serial numbers and a space for the owner's name and address.

GIGAKU

The vibrant Gigaku make-up range was inspired by the historical theatrical performances of Buddhist processional dances that were introduced to Japan in the early 7th century. Gigaku is thought to have originated in the central Chinese kingdom of Wu—known as 'Go' in Japanese, hence Gogaku, or 'music of Go'. However, some believe its true roots lie further west or in southwest Asia. Ancient texts indicate that the tradition arrived in Japan in 612, and is said to have been introduced by a Korean musician named Mimashi.

The popularity of Gigaku increased along with the spread of Buddhism and added some theatrical vibrancy to long Buddhist ceremonies. The actors would wear large decorative masks with exaggerated features as they acted out stories through dance and mime. Stan, Mark and Rowena travelled to London to watch a performance and were inspired by its energy and colours.

In true Cosmetics to Go fashion, what emerged was unique and unlike anything you could expect to find at a conventional make-up counter. Eye shadows and blushers were set into triangular segments of plaster, fitting together like pizza slices in a circular box so the customer could create their own bespoke pallet. Once again, Rowena found herself working over the weekend to perfect the packaging, meticulously pouring plaster of Paris into moulds.

As the make-up range expanded, so did the innovation in its packaging. Lavender blossoms and pastel colours were mixed into the plaster, making each segment as stunning as the shades it was housing.

Eventually, production of the segments were taken over by local artisans at Poole Pottery, freeing up Rowena to unleash her creativity onto the next project.

Gigaku Mascara was an old-fashioned solid block of pure colour and came in a red tin with its own brush and a mirror in the lid. You needed to wet the block to moisten the solid mascara and then use the provided brush to stroke the colour onto your eyelashes. Pre-empting the inevitable, the box came with a sticker on it saying 'Don't spit!'.

One of the colours was named after Stan. He was key to the range because he taught the team how to develop and manufacture make-up. Krysztal was a cool blue eye shadow and the catalogue notes it as being named after the 'cleverest colour cosmetician'. The work that Stan and Rowena had done on the Mistress's Lipstick for Forces Favourite became a part of this range too.

The range grew over the years and by catalogue #11 it had its own forty-eight page supplement printed on extremely shiny white paper to show the colours in their true glory.

GINGER
Eau De Parfum

'WARM RICH SCENT.'
Carole Oakes - Kings Acre, Hereford.

The Ginger perfume was one of Cosmetic to Go's most popular fragrances.

Like the company itself, Ginger was designed to be unique and distinctive. A spicy and warming ginger oil base cushioned a delicate floral blend of jasmine, rose and mimosa that combined to become an iconic smell...

'Love the smell, good enough to eat in a sensual sort of a way.' Julie Grundy - Selston, Notts.

Crate Inspiration!

After a company night out Mark and Mo dropped in to visit Rowena's new house. While she played hostess and offered them both a cup of tea, they noticed she was spooning the tea leaves from a beautifully painted wooden box made to look like a tiny tea crate. This innocuous item was to become the inspiration for the Ginger perfume packaging.

The crates had to be as beautiful as the perfume and many a weekend saw Rowena crawling up and down the length of the 12 Market Street office with rubber stamps and tubes of paint. This was where she would arrange a huge row of crates and meticulously stamp them all by hand.

Each crate required four separate stamps in a certain order to get the colourful Ginger logo just right, so it was a time-consuming exercise.

The Ginger fragrance was very successful at Cosmetics to Go and remained a best seller. It still pops up from time to time in the Lush Retro range too.

'One of the most evocative fragrances I have ever encountered.'
Maggie Michael - Little Chalfont, Bucks.

'everybody wants to know "what's that wonderful smell?"'
Karen Powell - Bradley Stoke North, Bristol.

'Ginger - because I get so many nice comments when I wear it.' Anon

The Ginger customer experience began at the front door... The crate turned up at their doorstep in a waft of exquisite fragrance because the perfume bottle was carefully packaged, nestled in delicious, ginger-smelling pot-pourri. A thoughtful touch that added to the olfactory experience!

We believe that this was the world's first perfume that focused on ginger as the main fragrance note.

Ginger | 73

Brown
The eponymously named Brown perfume.

Jeff Brown
1944-2001

Swelegant
Light and green with heady ylang ylang, sandalwood and a clove bud heart. Swelegant was elegance personified. Lah di dah!

To Know Me Is To Love Me

The inventors at Cosmetics to Go needed a professional perfumer to concoct fragrances for all their creations.

Previously Mark had worked with a perfumer named Jeff Brown, but when he went to find him where they had last worked together, he discovered he had left. Mark tracked him down to Brighton, where he was running an antiques shop in the Lanes.

Mark knew that Jeff was really great at perfumery. His previous work with fragrances at Constantine & Weir had led to best-selling products. The problem was that he was also really great at selling antiques, and he enjoyed it too.

Himalaya
'*One whiff transports you to the top of the world,*' said Rowena of this fragrance.

Elder
Elder was a response to customers requesting a light but long-lasting fragrance. Elderberry scented this bright herbal perfume.

Salarum
Inspired by a visit to the south of France, Salarum captured the sensation of walking along a salty beach in the fresh sea breeze. In 2019 this perfume was briefly resurrected in Lush, named Salarium, to celebrate the opening of the new Liverpool Lush anchor shop.

After some persuasion he agreed to help Cosmetics to Go with their perfumes. He set up a little lab in the basement of his antiques shop, and he and Mark worked together on getting the fragrances right for the products.

The Cosmetics to Go brand and range grew rapidly and Jeff found himself getting busier. The antiques business began to take a back seat and eventually he had so many perfumery assignments to work on that he set up his own business called Quintessence, purely to service them.

Following the success of the Ginger fragrance, he went on to develop a men's fragrance that would be an antithesis to all the vulgar, unashamed, 'power perfumes' that abounded in the 80s.

When he showed the new scent to Mark, he gave a rather understated presentation. Mark asked him bluntly, '*Well, what do you think? Do YOU like it?*' Jeff shrugged and replied,

> *It's alright, I wouldn't put my name on it.*

The perfume was promptly named 'Brown' and placed in Cosmetics to Go catalogue #2.

29½
Originally released as an exclusive fragrance only on sale in the Cosmetics to Go shop in Poole.

Pas De Musque
Cosmetics to Go had a strict no animal-testing policy*, but were still concerned about the prevalent use of musk in the perfume industry. This scent was devised to emphasise their stance, *en français naturellement.*

*see page 58–59

Trinity
The smell of a big bundle of blooms alongside the mouthwatering fragrance of Belgian chocolates. Divine!

Purrfume
A sophisticated black kitty adorned this pot of perfume that was designed to hark back to the glamorous 1950s. The muse for this fragrance was Doris Day.

Elemental
Inspired by the four elements – Earth, Air, Fire and Water.

Hollyhocks

Range for Men

Men's hollyhocks range - effective against male stereotyping.
Aileen Ingham - Withington, Manchester

Allow us to introduce the Hollyhocks range. A worthy successor to the now retired Khufu range, this was a determinedly feminine and floral bright new pretender, challenging the common perception of what it was to be manly.

Tough luck for all tough lads! Cosmetics to Go were anything but typical and overturning the macho stereotype was the objective.

The Hollyhocks range was beautiful to behold. Each product was bottled in brown glass with über-floral labels extolling the virtues of the product line for those who liked to pamper themselves. The labels playfully claimed that these products were for MEN ONLY! but, of course, that didn't stop everyone else getting their hands on them.

This range also featured Hothouse Steam Cream, a shaving cream that was made by infusing the ingredients with a shot of steam. When Mark was inventing this, he used the staff coffee machine to provide the steam and experimented with the effects of it on essential oils. After a while people grew wary of accepting the offer of a cup of coffee from him, as you were never quite sure what it would taste like!

> *Overturning the macho stereotype was the objective.*

This vivid, floral Paul Smith shirt, as modelled here by Mark with his daughter Claire, inspired all the labels and branding for the Hollyhocks range.

The Hollyhocks range featured moisturisers at a time when most men only used shaving cream and aftershave in their morning routines. Rowena reminisces that Clay was particularly lovely as the clay base would mattify the skin and get rid of any greasy glow.

Dudley, Chris and Ken

At this time, the word 'pansy' was often used in a derogatory way, and as a homophobic slur. Naming the perfume Pansy was a way to subvert and challenge this, and to focus on fragrance for everyone.

Hollyhocks Perfumes

The Hollyhocks range eschewed aftershave. Why fling alcohol onto sore, just-scraped, tender skin? In place of this they provided perfumed essences and a soft alcohol fragrance for men to be used for the scent, not the sting!

Narcissus – Named after the mythical Narcissus, an intoxicating incense and citrus scent for the man who hates to be parted from his mirror…

Rockery – The warm, sensual, resinous one of the range.

Hay – A reincarnation of Salarum took its place in the Hollyhocks range under the new name, Hay. The smell of a sea breeze on a salty shore.

Pansy* – Provocatively named and pleasantly reminiscent of childhood summer holidays, smelling of sweet blackberries and fruit gums.

Bramble – This fragrance featured a gentle, soft, sweet patchouli and blackcurrant scent.

* This fragrance lives on! Next time you are in Lush, have a sniff of The Olive Branch shower gel to see what it smelled like.

This is a photograph of one of the many frames full of customer pictures that Cosmetics to Go used to decorate their offices. As well as cheering up the offices they also reminded the staff of who they were working for.

The Cosmetics to Go mailbag encompassed much more than just comments on products and service. The office would receive letters and photos daily. Customers liked to send pictures of themselves using the products, as well as images of their partners, babies, children and animals!

This photo of Bronx Blonde Shampoo Bar user Malcolm and his friend Denise was sent in with the following pithy comment from her *'Another favourite with the blonde tart – I think he just likes the name of these things.'* This is one of Mark's all-time favourite customer comments, which appeared in catalogue #9.

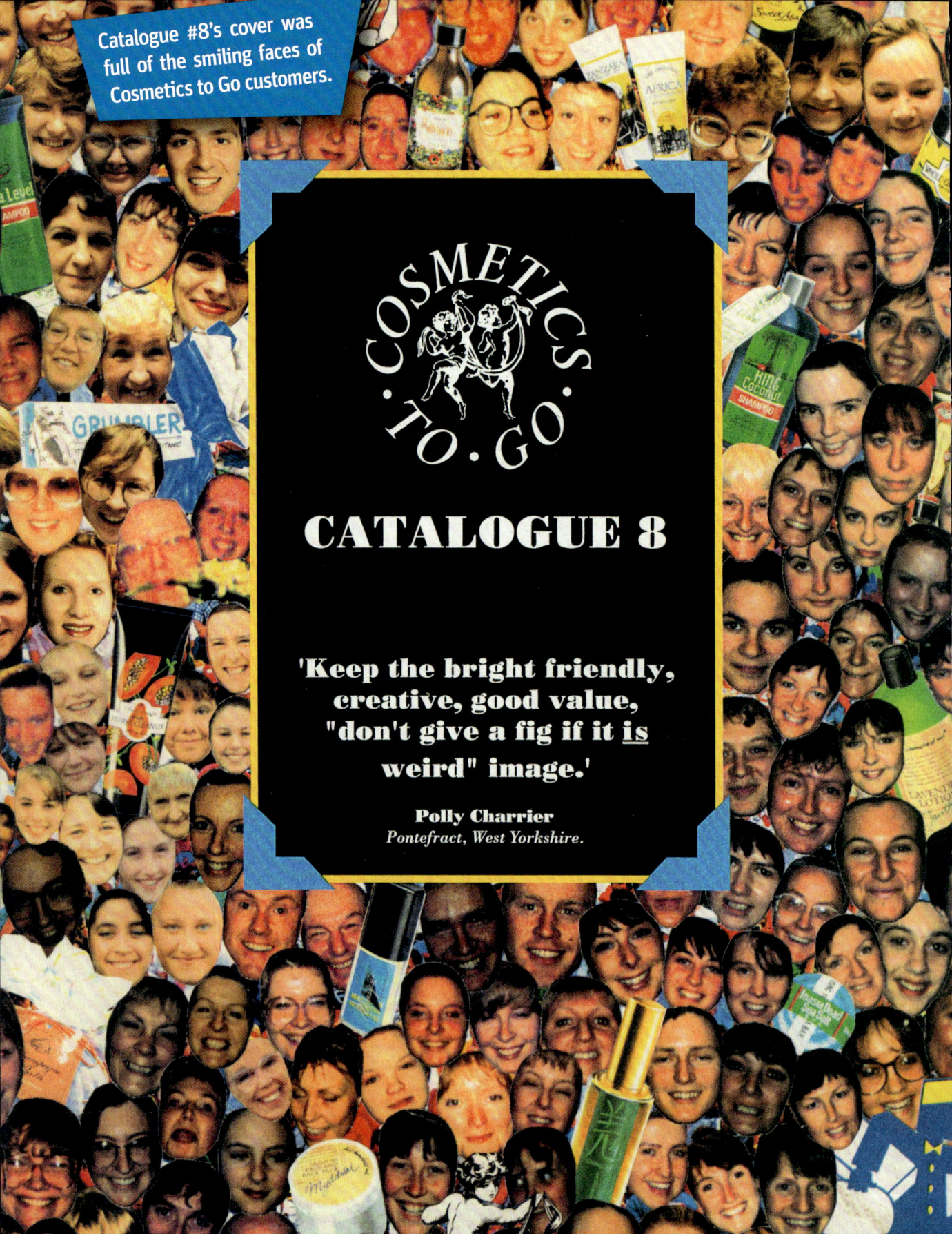

Sarah McCartney

Steve and Jo

Mrs T. Nicholson

Something Borrowed, Something Blue...

In 1992, Sarah McCartney was married and sent in photographs of her happy day. She included some scenic shots, too, and entitled the set 'Sky, Sea and My Wedding'.

Mark adored the photographs, loving her Audrey Hepburn-inspired look, and decided to include this romantic montage of pictures in catalogue #9.

The floodgates opened and brides up and down the country began to send in photographs of themselves in all their bridal glory. Many of the catalogues would go on to feature these happy couples.

Sarah was a loyal fan of Cosmetics to Go right from the start. She would later become the writer and editor of the *Lush Times*, aka Auntie Pamela.

'Less Waffle and more facts'

Catalogues had a fan-club feel, with correspondence always included, even when the comments received were not flattering...

Complaints were often featured in the catalogues. The company would publish their apologies alongside and explain the steps being taken to fix the problems.

Customer satisfaction was such a priority that catalogue #4's opening page was a long letter from a customer with a list of grumbles. This letter was proudly presented on the front page before even the slightest mention of any products.

They tried to make customers' wishes and dreams come true too. A customer wrote in wishing that cosmetics firms would be more forthcoming about the ingredients they were using. Cosmetics to Go decided to include quantitative ingredient lists so customers knew exactly what was going into each product. One of the Ten Company Rules was to value and serve customers, and quite often Cosmetics to Go would be guided by the voice of the customer too.

Whatever it is... It's All About You...

'Sorry to be pedantic... but this drives me mad! One lays the table, or even eggs but you LIE in the bath..'

The Pen Is Mightier Than The Sword...

'Dear Cosmetics To Go,
Just writing to say that you have some lovely dovely stuff, as always, BUT, as we are only poor GCSE students, basically, WE CAN NOT AFFORD IT. What happened to the small tubs, tubes and bottles that only fetched a measly, but very affordable to us folk, £1.50ish? Please, please, please...'

Rebekah Morley-Jones, Powys... full of comments and suggestions... feverishly...

"I wish I could accept criticism as you do. It's done you good though because this catalogue is much better than the last."

Luv - Fiona Shone, Blaenau Ffestiniog

Printed in England   Printed on recycled paper

Cosmetics to Go staff were reputed to work hard and party harder. We found a few shots of the gorgeous crew on best behaviour at company conferences and at play for your delectation!

THE TEN COMPANY RULES

Value people before profit

Opportunity hangs in the air

Develop and promote talent from within

Take responsibility for our environment

and serve customers

VALUE

TECHNOLOGY
Benefit from the use of new technology

The Ten Company Rules reflected the beliefs and principles of the company, as they were created through consultation with everyone who worked there. Each member of staff had their own personal copy of the rules. Some of them still carry them today.

Lush customers may recognise some of these rules, as they form the basis of the beliefs and values that are still held at Lush in the form of the We Believe statement.

'We need to care about each other and help others'

Christmas to Go

Rudolph Bomb not only looked cute as could be, but also fizzed an aromatherapy blend to cure hangovers!

Being a member of staff at Cosmetics to Go was a little like being part of a large and rather eccentric family.

It became a seasonal tradition that every Christmas Eve morning, Mark would cook a huge fry up for everyone. All the staff were invited, as well as friends of the company.

Christmas Eve breakfasts were also a time to celebrate surviving the busy Christmas retail period. It was a good time to relax, unwind and, most importantly, celebrate!

Hot Toddy was a spicy cinnamon and clove-scented bath that made the whole house smell like Christmas! This product has remained a Christmas tradition and sometimes seasonally sneaks onto the shelves of Lush!

Simon Constantine

Relaxing with workmates

88 | Cosmetics to Go

Cheers Tony!

Snowman Soap was a huge best seller but a nightmare to manufacture. His carrot soap nose would break off inside the mould and would have to be reattached using soldering irons – a very fiddly and time-consuming task!

Mark opening the fizz

This beatific gift contained two heavenly bath bombs that tumbled into the tub in a froth of shimmering effervescence. The creative team added white soap flakes to the mix so the bath would lather as well as fizz for a Christmas night double delight.

Christmas to Go | 89

Looking After the People

Way back in the early Constantine & Weir days, lots of product formulation took place at Mark and Mo's house. At lunchtime the work would stop and Mo would prepare lunch for everybody. This was normally Heinz tomato soup and crackers and was eaten around the family kitchen table.

Karl remembers this as being handy when money was tight. You could turn up to work with no cash in your pockets or the bank, but know that you were going to get fed.

As the company grew, and became Cosmetics to Go, they still wanted to take the same care of the people who worked for them, even as the workforce expanded.

To this end, they provided kitchens in the factory and offices. Staff could come in and have breakfast and lunch at the factory.

A factory 'Mum' was hired to buy in bags and bags of food shopping so that the cupboards were always full. The Mum also made homemade tray bakes and cakes for people to enjoy. Full tummies meant happier workers!

As well as food for everybody at work, washing machines and tumble dryers were also available. When you started your shift you could pop your wash in and have a freshly laundered set of clothes by the end of it.

If you wanted to head straight out of the factory to go out on the town then you could take a shower and scrub up using Cosmetics to Go products.

Not only this, but if you had a special occasion and wanted to look especially primped, or even if you just needed a trim, there was an onsite hairdresser. Perfect for those bad hair days.

Alex wears Tartlet by Cosmetics to Go

Some of the Cosmetics to Go employees lived in the villages and towns surrounding Poole. The shifts started very early and public transport could be unreliable. How did Cosmetics to Go remedy this? Simple, a fleet of white Citroën cars were given to certain members of staff to use. If anyone else needed to get somewhere quickly they could borrow the keys and hop in.

Local Poole residents got used to the distinctive cars whizzing about and some customers got to experience them too, as they would be used to ferry visitors from the shop to the factory.

Many of the team would socialise in the Angel Pub at the end of Market Street after work. The youthful workforce worked and played together. The company helped sociability rise to decadent and debaucherous levels with shopping and dinner trips to London either hiring coaches or taking over train carriages courtesy of British Rail.

There were often pranks and frivolity on these trips. In particular Mark sneaking a can of silly string onto the train at Poole and giggling to himself, only to arrive into the carriage assailed by a blizzard of silly string as every single person seated in there had been given a can. '*I was covered in the stuff!*' he laughed, '*And so was the entire carriage!*'

When a hapless magician was hired to entertain the troops at a fancy restaurant, he provided more entertainment than he had bargained for when his monkey puppet was stolen as everybody left to board the bus home. Liz climbed up to the top deck to witness the unlucky furry puppet being thrown around in a drunken game of catch. It promptly disappeared as her head emerged at the top of the stairs. '*Come on you lot!*' she said, '*We have to give the man his monkey back.*' Eventually, it was truculently passed over…

Looking After the People

The Factory

The Cosmetics to Go team had to overhaul their entire manufacturing department when they started production of their own products. The transition was made from supplying tonnes of Body Shop formulas to more specialised products in smaller quantities for their own customers.

New machines were tooled specifically for the unique requirements of Cosmetics to Go. The gleaming stainless-steel machines that arrived enabled the teams to make up more complicated formulas containing all manner of natural ingredients and essential oils.

Sharon Etherington and Maxine James, who kindly shared their memories of working in the factory, recalled that huge amounts of fruit and vegetables were regularly delivered to the factory to be used in the products. It was important to prepare this fresh produce quickly. Part of the job was to get it all ready to go into the mixing vessels as soon as possible.

The factory was a fast-paced environment. It had to be run extremely efficiently as it was the sole provider of every single cosmetic listed in the catalogues. There were so many different products that staff had to be extremely versatile, fast and organised. It could be a highly stressful environment at times, as the pressure was always on to ensure that supply kept up with demand.

Local companies supported the factory and took products off site to bottle, package and deliver. Friends and family of Cosmetics to Go ran some of these. Pictured below are Tony Sanders of Three Counties Packaging, Ashley Rogers of Ashpack and Ann Rogers of Rogers' Wrap & Pack.

Steve mixing product

The raw material arrives

Tony Sanders of Three Counties Packaging

A moment of calm for Ashley of Ashpack

Ann Rogers of Rogers' Wrap & Pack shows off a Bombastic

STORY

Karl mixes up bespoke batches

Karl

One of Mark and Mo's first employees, Karl worked making products in their kitchen. Discovering that he was so skint that he was paying for food on his credit card started the tradition of ensuring that all staff were fed (see page 90). Keeping him well nourished proved to be a good investment as he grew with the company to take on pivotal roles and eventually became a director.

to swap valves and tubes at the bottom. If the radio was playing at its usual level and if the mood took you, people were known to use the paddles and electrical parts as play microphones for a bit of light relief. You had to be careful leaving this machine unattended, though, as a few unlucky people discovered when they went off for breaks. If no one was there to switch parts around when it started beeping, it would simply pump whatever it was mixing all over the floor.

At crucial times in the factory, everyone was all business. In the most hectic production periods, before Christmas or for a sale, it was all hands on deck. People would come from the shop and offices to join in and help out.

At the end of a long factory shift, most of the crew would head to the Angel Inn to have drinks, socialise and blow off steam.

There was definitely a sense of 'work hard, play hard'. With the number of young people working in the factory there was a very playful energy. There was always music blaring from the radio. Despite attempts to keep the music levels low, the tunes were still blasted out. With all the fresh produce hanging around, fruit fights were sometimes known to break out, and in the free for all it was important to watch out for a flying tomato or banana!

Even day-to-day tasks in the pressured environment could be made fun. The contrablend machine, for example, was a spherical device that looked like a space vehicle. Its job was to emulsify solutions between two large chambers, and this involved pumping one solution across to the other using huge spanners

Factory Tours

'It's not every day that you look at your bar of soap and think, gosh, I'd love to know how they made that...'

Cosmetics to Go were proud of the factory and all the magic that happened there. The team were also aware from all the lovely fan mail and chatty phone calls from customers that people really were invested in a relationship with the company.

Customers visiting...

Behind the scenes

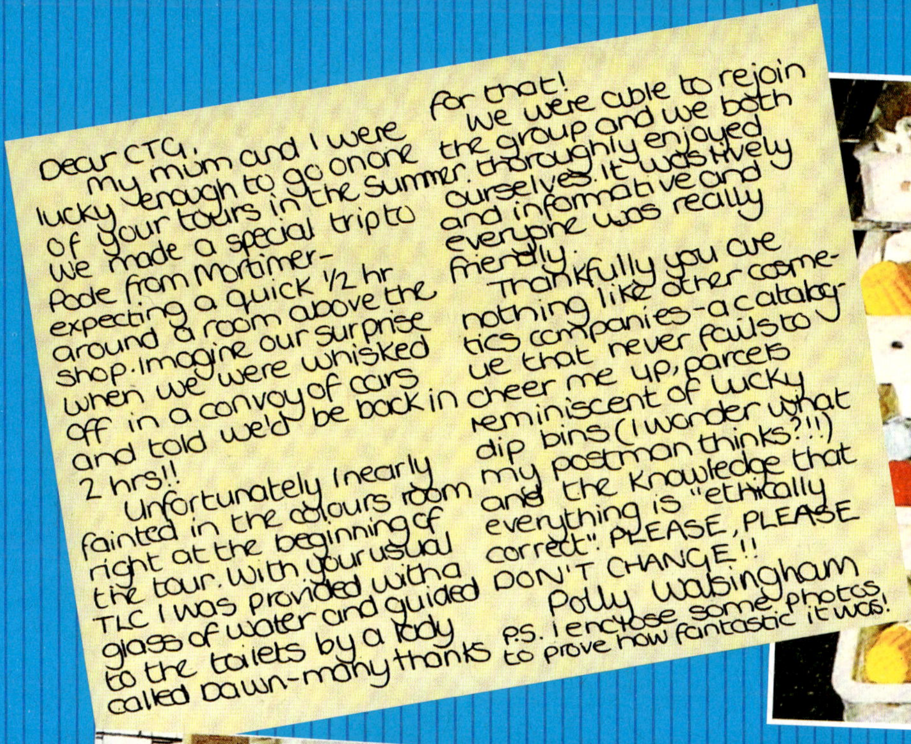

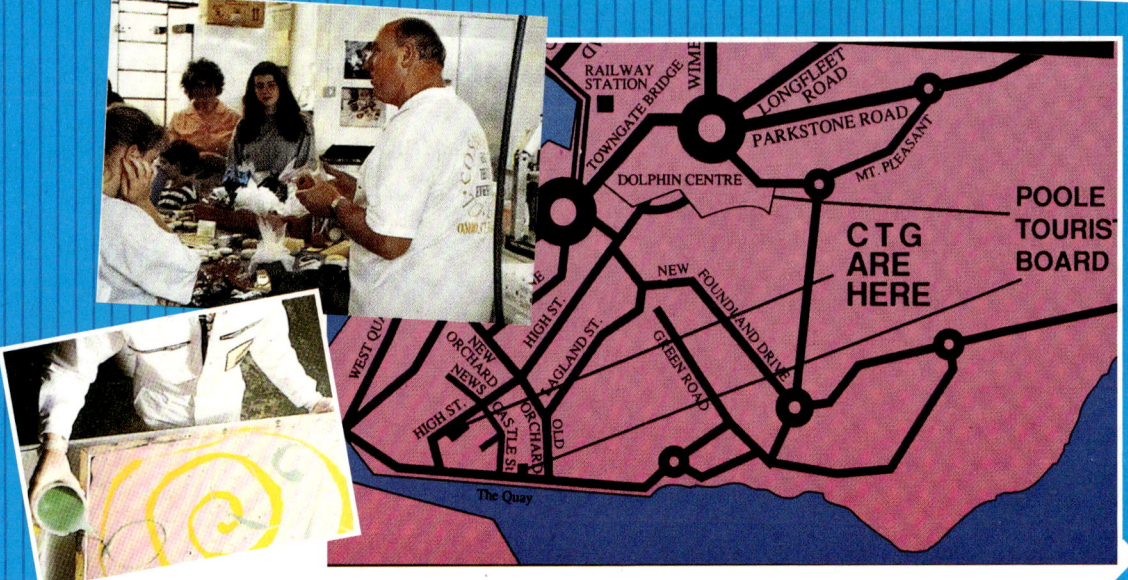

> Dear CTG,
> My mum and I were lucky enough to go on one of your tours in the summer. We made a special trip to Poole from Mortimer-expecting a quick 1/2 hr around a room above the shop. Imagine our surprise when we were whisked off in a convoy of cars and told we'd be back in 2 hrs!!
> Unfortunately I nearly fainted in the colours room right at the beginning of the tour. With your usual TLC I was provided with a glass of water and guided to the toilets by a lady called Dawn—many thanks for that! We were able to rejoin the group and we both thoroughly enjoyed ourselves. It was lively and informative and everyone was really friendly.
> Thankfully you are nothing like other cosmetics companies—a catalogue that never fails to cheer me up, parcels reminiscent of lucky dip bins (I wonder what my postman thinks?!!) and the knowledge that everything is "ethically correct". PLEASE, PLEASE DON'T CHANGE!!
> Polly Walsingham
> P.S. I enclose some photos to prove how fantastic it was!

It seemed to make perfect sense for Cosmetics to Go to open their factory doors and show off what went on within. This way fans could get a glimpse behind the scenes and see how all their favourite products were made. A true Willy Wonka, golden ticket experience.

During the summer months, a Cosmetics to Go minibus would pick up eager fans from Poole station or the shop at 29 High Street and take them along to the factory. Once there they were guided inside, where they got to see the products being compounded, witness the cruelty-free human tests taking place, have a glimpse into the Gigaku colour room and really get a feel for how things worked. The handmade nature of the Cosmetics to Go products meant that staff were always available to chat with customers while products were being made.

The factory team were dedicated to keeping things interesting and entertaining. Sure enough, there were a few surprises in store for visitors that added to the experience... not things you'd find in your common or garden type factory anyway!

CTG at *The Clothes Show Live*

As well as bringing the public to the factory, Cosmetics to Go decided to take the factory to the public!

The Clothes Show Live event featured the hottest fashion labels and cosmetic companies and the newest trends were displayed for the public. Fashion disciples would make the pilgrimage to the Birmingham NEC to find out what would be the next big thing and to see the next season's new looks before everybody else.

Cosmetics to Go's aim at the event was to pick up as many new customers as possible and to build the mailing list. New names and addresses were vital to grow the customer base and advance the business. As a company, they did not pay for advertising campaigns so these kind of events were relied on for exposure to the public and the pressure was always on to collect as many new fans as possible.

Martin Bachell & Jim Dobbs getting it all ready

Kitchen demo area

Round the back...

Helen demonstrated the Filboid Studge Wheatgrass Cleanser being made by snipping wheatgrass growing in troughs on the counter and whizzing it up with clay, cocoa butter and essential oils. This was possibly the crowd's first experience of literal step-up-to-the-window and grab your freshly made Cosmetics to Go!

In true Cosmetics to Go style, they decided to have the biggest and best stand. A well-appointed corner stand was made to look as if the shop and factory had been built at the exhibition, complete with steam (in the form of dry ice) and live compounding so people could see the products being made right in front of their eyes

Martin Bachell, a set designer that Jeff Osment had conscripted, created a virtual storefront with a wide counter where people could watch all that was going on inside. No expense was spared and it was well worth it. The stand became the place to be and streams of people came to see these bright young things ply their trade and explain all their wacky and wonderful products.

The event was televised on BBC1 as a special *Clothes Show Live* programme. The presenters spent time at the stand enraptured by the demonstration of a speedy metamorphosis of wheatgrass and a few ingredients into an instant cosmetic face mask. When the show transmitted, Cosmetics to Go were featured. Up and down the country viewers scribbled down the company's details to send off for their catalogues.

The producers of the programme adored the stand and the company, and were keen to meet up to talk about featuring them on the television show in their own slot. This was a huge break for the company as it meant that they would get some real airtime.

This first jaunt to Birmingham was pronounced a huge success. The team brought back bundles of names and addresses, some great photographs and stories of the event and a secured spot on *The Clothes Show*. Spirits were high. It was decided to plan for a return and an even bigger, better appearance next year.

This drawing was the original illustration that Cosmetics to Go designer and carpenter Martin Bachell provided when the team asked him for a stand designed to look like a real shop. You can see how faithfully this was reproduced in the photograph. It caused quite the stir at the event.

CTG at The Clothes Show Live

CTG on TV

The Clothes Show transmitted on a Sunday evening right after the news on BBC1 and regularly pulled in huge viewing figures.

The production team came to Poole to learn more about the company and plan their slot on the show. Following a quick tour and fact-finding mission they decided the best place to show off all these exciting, never-before-seen items like the bath bombs, was in action in a bathroom... and who had the perfect bath? Happily, Mark and Mo did at their house.

This was how it came to pass that Jeff Banks, the face and main presenter of *The Clothes Show*, and his film crew crowded into Mark's bathroom around the gleaming white bathtub. They were about to film a televisual first – the onscreen debut of the bath bomb. The cameras started to roll, as Jeff sat perched on the side of the bath watching a Blackberry Bath Bomb explode in the water. The camera closed up on the Boom Boom message that emerged from the fizz.

Jeff Banks went on to interview Mark and Helen, asking questions about the Cosmetics to Go range, and was also filmed visiting the factory while they made Christmas products. Helen took the opportunity to talk about the company's stance on animal testing. The whole piece featured the products heavily and was a fabulous introduction of the brand to many viewers. The show that evening pulled in 5.9 million viewers. It was a great coup for Cosmetics to Go to be featured.

Indeed, the Cosmetics to Go staff seemed very at home in the limelight and television offers came flooding in.

Mark, Helen and Rowena were all regularly asked to appear as guests to comment on the fields that they specialised in. This helped boost their reputation as beauty and bathing experts and ensured they were always in demand when cosmetic topics came up!

CTG on TV | 99

Generation Game

Despite the presenter trying to eat the ingredients, Rowena demonstrated how to put together an edible face mask for the contestants to try their hand at it, with varying results!

Rowena keeps cool in front of a studio audience

The Time The Place

Cosmetics to Go staff enjoyed being interviewed on discussion shows as experts in cosmetics. In this episode of *The Time The Place*, Mark discussed perfume.

The Time The Place evidently!

Mark explains how men should wear perfume

Wire TV

Rowena took an opportunity to display Cosmetics to Go wares on cable entertainment channel Wire TV. A range of products from bath bombs to face masks got airtime and she even managed to show off the iconic Cosmetics to Go parcel!

Rowena & presenter

Rowena demos the iconic Cosmetics to Go box

Going Live

This popular Saturday morning kids TV show filmed a segment with Mark at *The Clothes Show*, letting a legion of younger fans in on the Cosmetics to Go goodies.

Preamble and a vista of the exhibition stands

Interviewing Mark for the Saturday morning viewers

WAKE UP WITH ROWENA

Beetroot blusher ably demonstrated

Rowena & Paula contemplate hairy legs

No excuse for stinky feet, Andi!

Bemused boyband get facials

Cosmetics to Go novelty showercap in full effect

ON THE BIG BREAKFAST!

The Big Breakfast was the wildly popular breakfast show that millions of Britons woke up to for a technicoloured morning. A perfect fit, Cosmetics to Go were invited to come along to talk about their products. Not only this, Rowena became their beauty expert for a week and a contributor to their regular Super-Hints feature!

In her time on *The Big Breakfast* she explained how to make face masks, hair masks and make-up from kitchen ingredients alongside the effervescent Paula Yates. She also found time to anoint kids TV presenter Andi Peters with a foot mask and even managed to get face masks onto the reluctant members of bad boy pop act East 17.

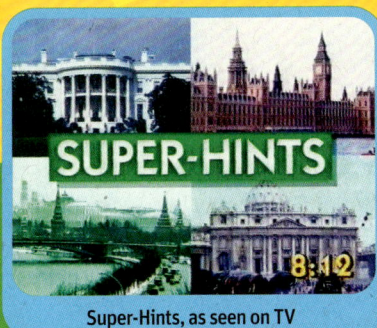
Super-Hints, as seen on TV

Rowena dispenses wisdom to the nation

Read All About It

Janis Raven, Head of Bubble Publicity, was Cosmetic to Go's effervescent public relations agent.

She regularly managed to secure column inches across national and local press, beauty magazines and industry publications. She also courted the television channels and made sure that onscreen appearances were so frequent that the team began to feel quite at home in front of the cameras.

The company policy of not paying to advertise meant that press exposure was crucial in keeping Cosmetics to Go current and talked about. The amount of press that Janis was able to secure for this relatively small cosmetics firm was phenomenal. Here is a selection of some of the press that we have exhumed from the archives and dusted off for your delectation.

Janis

Fight for labelling of cosmetic ingredients

BY JOANNA CODD

THE latest catalogue by Poole-based Cosmetics to Go is out now – complete with a plea to its customers.

CTG supremo Mark Constantine wants everyone to bombard their Euro MPs with letters supporting the compulsory labelling of cosmetics ingredients.

At the moment, customers can unwittingly buy products to which they may be allergic or have moral objections.

Cosmetics to Go, which operates from Poole High Street, is backing the current campaign by the British Association of Dermatologists by fully labelling seven of its ranges.

None of the innovative company's products is tested on animals. All of it is acceptable for vegetarians and some – specially marked with a tick in the catalogue – is suitable for vegans.

The sixth CTG catalogue features 52 pages of products. New ranges include Hollyhocks – a mix of flowers and

Bournemouth Evening Echo 17 August 1990

MY BIGGEST MISTAKE
Mark Constantine

Mark Constantine, 40, is managing director of Cosmetics to Go. He developed his interest in cosmetics while still at school, when he became involved with theatrical make-up. He trained as a hairdresser, then applied for a job as a television make-up artist. Meanwhile, he had developed an interest in ecology and natural history. On moving from London to Dorset, he set up a business with wife Mo and Liz Weir, making natural cosmetics for other companies, such as the Body Shop, before launching the current mail-order company five years ago.

The Independent on Sunday 12 September 1993

> I make mistakes on a regular basis, but I'm learning from them. It is difficult to pick the worst, but perhaps it is the most recent one.
>
> We built the business from a £100 start in my bedroom to a £6m-7m turnover, initially by producing cosmetics and selling them to other companies.
>
> Then, about five years ago, we had lots of ideas that those companies didn't want. So we put them in a catalogue and called it "Cosmetics to Go". After a while, we decided to concentrate on this side.
>
> We have had problems coping with the massive growth. This has important effects on stock. Last Christmas we did not have enough, yet in the New Year we had some left over.
>
> But when you expand a business you must have stock. You either hang on to it or you have a sale. Normally we have dealt with this by having a discount book, so that customers can get older products at lower prices. But this year we decided to issue a 48-page full sale catalogue in July.
>
> Our phone room can handle 18,000 calls a week and process 3,000 orders a day. But in no time we were receiving 9,000 to 10,000 calls a day. In July we had 100,000 orders – 80,000 by post and 20,000 by phone. On 12 Ju-

we had more than 40,000 unfilled orders. It was the worst thing that could have happened.

The computer company claims ours is the only one of its systems to have crashed – and it may be right. But in one week we couldn't answer 130,000 calls. We reckon we missed 9,000 orders and 7,000 catalogue requests. No one knew if we were in business or not.

Because some orders were dispatched without being computerised, the phone room could not tell callers whether goods had been sent out.

We got the computer going again within 48 hours. But we lost nearly all the August sales – about £700,000 – because we were processing requests from the previous month.

We are obviously more popular than we realised. And at least it didn't happen at Christmas, a critical time, because so many people buy our products as presents.

We have ordered a new telephone system with double the number of lines and have a mirrored computer system, so that if there's a problem we can continue.

The problem highlighted the importance of assessing correctly the demand for your products.

Over-trading is the single largest threat to the entre-

YAHOO! IT'S A NEW CATALOGUE FROM COSMETICS TO GO!

And it's got a rather attractive psychedelic cover! Within these groovy pages there's zillions of brilliant make-up, creams, perfumes, shampoos, conditioners, soaps and other things fab enough to make your

Jackie 27 April 1991

The Times 13 February 1991

THE TIMES

Independent on Sunday
[De]cember 1993

By Helen Hague

GET catalogues that look [like] doorstops and offer shop [goods] by post on tick. A new [form] of mail-order retailing has [been] changing the face of arm[chair] shopping.

It started in the US but is [s]preading here. Take two com[p]anies that started small and [h]ave boomed as others have gone bust.

Last week, Mark Constantine, of Cosmetics To Go, was pushing his product at the Clothes Show Live exhibition, decked out in plastic angel wings, moving niftily amid clouds that festooned the companies' stand.

It is not the conventional behaviour of a managing director, but Cosmetics To Go, of Poole, Dorset, is not a conventional company. It uses zany, pun-spattered catalogues to sell its products. Take your pick from Christmas gift sets: It's Frosty, Man; I Snow Him So Well; Snowing Me, Snowing You. Get the drift?

The catalogue has achieved cult status in certain quarters and is designed to hang around. "We did think of putting a hole in the top so you could hang it by the loo. People should browse through it."

A recent promotion asked customers to nominate friends who would be sent free bath bombs through the post. It took off more spectacularly than Mr Constantine had expected. "We thought about 70,000 people would take it up. In the event, 270,000 did."

But Cosmetics To Go has found that its policy of sending "freebies" through the post, followed up by a catalogue, is building up a client list and paying dividends.

Research shows that nearly four in five of the company's customers are affluent urban couples or house-sharers aged 25 to 44.

Selling should be fun — so when Mr Constantine was asked by Radio One if he would do a live make-up session for a transvestite customer as part of the station's Clothes Show Live coverage, he was happy to oblige. It turned out that the man had spent £200 on Cosmetics To Go products the week before. He first got to hear of the company when a champagne bath bomb arrived through the post. Positive proof that spreading the product by spreading fun pays dividends.

"The pleasure of Cosmetics To Go is that we make the kind of products we want to," says Mr Constantine, a herbalist and trichologist.

Growth has been phenomenal — building up from a £100 start in Mr Constantine's bedroom to a £6m-£7m turnover. Taking a break from his stand,

Mr Constantine talks business. "This year we'll have done 10 times the turnover we did in 1989. We have received critical acclaim, but to say we are phenomenally successful suggests that we are making massive profits which we are not."

No cover-up

WITH more than a million people in the UK estimated to suffer from sensitivity to products used in cosmetics, it is welcome news that the mail-order make-up company Cosmetics to Go will be listing full ingredients on all its products by the end of this year, and is encouraging other manufacturers to follow suit. Cosmetics to Go's managing director, Mark Constantine, says: "Food manufacturers are no longer able to hide behind the mystique of the secret recipe . . . why deny the customer that same information about cosmetic ingredients?"

VICTORIA McKEE

Tatler September 1992

The Daily Telegraph 19 July 1993

Secrets of looking good enough to eat

Don't taste the purée: it goes on your face. **Hilary Alexander** on a cosmetics company with some odd ideas – and a catalogue to match

IN A SHOP in the seaside town of Poole, Dorset, customers stare into the glass display cabinet of what looks like a delicatessen counter. Fresh fruit, vegetables and herbs are arrayed on a bed of straw. An assistant, Tara Evans, mixes what is surely taramasalata in an earthenware bowl.

It looks good enough to eat, but that is the last thing you would do. Tomatoes are churned up with oil and vinegar, not for a dip, but a balm for tired feet; vitamin A-rich papaya is mashed with wheatgerm and turns into a cleanser; lemons, strawberries and ginger are puréed to make face packs.

The range, called The Fridge (because that is where you keep it), is just one of the ideas developed by Cosmetics To Go (CTG), the mail order beauty company.

Founder Mark Constantine, 40, established CTG in February 1988 with four other directors: his wife, Mo, Rowena Hofbauer, Helen Ambrosen and Karl Bygrave. The team previously operated as Constantine and Weir, makers of natural beauty products for the Body Shop and Czech & Speake.

The company is one of the success stories of the Eighties' "green" movement, with its eco-conscious generation prime targets for anything wrapped in brown paper and string. But customers are buying a concept as much as a product and Constantine is careful to ensure that the range, while it comes from the earth, does not promise it. Directions for using the soaps, creams and masks talk as much about the smell ("fills the air with the heavy and hypnotic scent of patchouli and geranium"; "might smell like creosote") as they do about the effect ("soothing", "gentle", "rich and calming").

Mr Constantine, a free spirit who pounds his Apple Mac to Fleetwood Mac and refuses to own a car, feels "there's almost too much romanticising about 'green' and 'natural' things. We don't want to fool the public. Some of our products, like The Fridge range, are 100 per cent natural. Others use modern preservatives, like methyl paraben, which enables a product to have a shelf-life. But these are safe and non-animal tested."

He has a soft spot for modern technology and sees no contradiction in using high-tech machinery to produce cosmetics based on 17th-century herbal remedies.

CTG is best known for its twice-yearly catalogue, which will be monthly from next month. It is a quirky, brightly coloured cross between a *Viz* comic and a cartoon strip, full of excruciating puns, snatches of philosophy and snapshots and poems sent in by customers. It has a circulation of 400,000 and a customer base of 200,000 who order from more than 200 items with an average price of £6-£7; prices start from £1-10.

The company employs 70 people (average age 23) on a job-sharing system; each swaps around, making bubble bath one month, answering the telephones the next.

BEHIND the wacky image, the company is fiercely opposed to animal testing. Mr Constantine began working with the British Union for Anti-Vivisection (BUAV) in the early Eighties. His team pioneered the "Assist Test" developed between 1986-88 by Haldane Laboratories in Poole. This is a humane method using cultures made from human skin cells gathered in 1975 and reproduced under laboratory conditions, instead of living creatures.

In 1991, CTG took its stance further, refusing to buy from any companies that test *any* of their raw materials on animals. Product safety is ensured with in-house testing; the day we visited, staff were trying quince-seed mascara (to soften and condition), lipstick made with goldenrod (helps prevent cold sores) and eyebright eyeliner (guards against conjunctivitis) — all based on traditional "hedgerow" remedies. More than 2,000 people in Poole and Bournemouth try out the finished products.

Three years ago CTG introduced Quantitative Ingredient Listings (a requirement in America since 1973) after consultation with the British Association of Dermatologists. The listing shows every item used — from oils and herbs to preservatives — so helping customers to make an informed choice.

"Food manufacturers cannot hide behind the mystique of the secret recipe," Mr Constantine says. "We all know what's in tomato ketchup, so why deny the customer the same information about cosmetic ingredients?"

□ *Cosmetics To Go; inquiries freefone 0800 373 366.*

Modern-day herbalists: Mark and Mo Constantine

Deeply dippy

Cosmetics To Go will deliver mail order madness to your home. Susan Irvine opens her post

A parcel arrives on the doorstep marked 'Very Important Package', it is covered in medieval engravings, cartoon strips and 'S.W.A.L.K.'. Inside are seven good reasons for not going to Boots: Dr Ozone Stranglehold Hairspray ('Trust me, I'm a doctor'); Happy Hippy Grapefruit Hair & Body Shampoo ('Mellow, yellow, with the fab smell of freshly squeezed grapefruits'); Dimestore Blonde Home Hairdye Kit; Product X Washing Powder – for your body, not your laundry; Pansy, the outrageously-named perfume for men; Fresh Herb Mask with pounded garlic (guaranteed to keep vampires and sane men at bay); and, best of all, the sexiest massage potion in the land – Knights in White Chocolate, its ingredients are about 75 per cent cocoa butter, 25 per cent white chocolate. Massage it on; lick it off.

'My ideal customer,' says Mark Constantine, 'is an upper-class type with private means who lives in a council house. You know, someone who escapes all those marketing men's stereotypes.' [...] describes the character of his mail [...] local growers await transformation, while Mrs Muggleton in 'Make-up' pots her eyeshadows the old-fashioned way, with a hand press.

Animal testing is a hot issue for Constantine. He worked with the British Union for the Abolition of Vivisection to introduce the five-year rule that ensures approved products contain no ingredients tested on animals in the last five years. 'When people ask me what British cosmetics are about, I say "cruelty-free". The British have a talent for caring about the wider issues.'

He was in at the beginning of the trend: 'I remember working with Beauty Without Cruelty. Founder Lady Dowding had the company's horoscope cast to ensure it was all under the right star.' His most famous association, however, was with Anita Roddick of The Body Shop. In Roddick's autobiography, she discovers Constantine living in the woods, creating products of mad cosmetic genius in his head. According to Constantine, it wasn't quite like that: 'I did [go] to Constantine [through] a wolf-boy phase but that was a few [...]

SETTING UP A LOCAL SHOP!

COSMETICS · TO · GO

"OH YEH!" HIGH PITCH "OOH!" ALL YEAR 'RAVE' AT COSMETICS TO GO

29 High Street was the centre of the Cosmetics to Go universe...

COME & TALK SHOP

Cosmetics to Go

Due to the agreement made with the Body Shop, Cosmetics to Go were not allowed to set up in direct competition with them as a high street retailer. They were, however, allowed to have a single shop to trade from, so the familiar environs of 29 High Street were transformed into a Cosmetics to Go shop decorated in bright colours and bursting full of products.

Once inside you could pop in for your favourite products, have a chat with whoever was working that day and find out all the gossip and news about what the company was up to. You could even wander through to a lab area, where the inventors would explain all about the new products they were developing as they were formulating them.

Inside 29 High Street!

104 | Cosmetics to Go

Helen sharing the knowledge

Rowena at the Radio One Roadshow

Cosmetics to Go also held talks and lectures to present what they were up to all over Britain. This was also a great opportunity to explain and show off the product range in local hotels and build relationships within a community.

Their hearts, however, belonged to Poole, and they were determined to please and go the extra mile for the Dorset locals. Local orders went through the shop and not the computer system in order to provide a truly personal, old-fashioned shopping experience. This was a nice touch, but could lead to issues in customer fulfilment. Orders were sometimes delivered twice, or not at all if the person taking the order had scribbled it down and lost the slip of paper. To make up for lost packages, Poole taxi drivers were called upon to deliver replacements directly to their homes if the Cosmetics to Go van was unavailable.

Some local customers were disappointed to find their names dropped from the Cosmetics to Go mailing list. This was because while they were receiving personal service from the shop, their purchases were not registered on the computerised mail-order system. After a period of inactivity, the system would delete them, thinking they were no longer interested. Devoted local shoppers would then miss out on new catalogues and loyalty rewards that mail-order customers would get automatically. Most notably, people were upset when repeat buying did not guarantee them the delivery of Ration Books, which contained vouchers and discounts. The very customers they were trying so hard to look out for were being penalised.

This was very typical of the Cosmetics to Go approach, all bright, good intentions with the heart in the right place, but falling down a little when it came to having systems in place making sure that things ran smoothly.

Helen demos the Below Zero armband

Mark passes out products

Setting up a Local Shop!

On the Champs-Élysées

Rowena and Helen on a visit to Nepal sourcing Rhododendron oil

Cosmetics to Global

Although Cosmetics to Go were based in the seaside town of Poole, England, their influences, ingredients and muses came from all over the globe.

Rowena and Helen were dispatched to Singapore on a mission to visit the orchid farms there. On another occasion, Jeff Brown accompanied them on a trip to Nepal. Travelling to the origin of the ingredients was a great privilege and they used these opportunities to learn about the native plants and their suppliers and gather as much information as they could.

Travellers were also prompted to take as many good photos of their trips as they could. Photographs from these locations provided great material for the catalogues.

Some of the travel destinations were closer to home. Marcia Davies, who wrote copy for the catalogue, was dispatched to investigate Myddfai in Wales and take some pictures to bring back for the Botanomancy pages (see pages 50–51). When she arrived in the small town it was a cold, wet, grey day and she was unable to get the picturesque scenes that she was hoping to capture.

Her next trip was to Ireland to take a seaweed bath to illustrate the beneficial properties of this ingredient.

sealevel

COSMETICS·TO·GO

The Sea Level range was inspired by the sea, salt and all things oceanic, but the start of this saline inspiration originally came from unexpected quarters...

The cosmetics industry was very interested in Cosmestics to Go. When it arrived on the scene it intrigued people with all the weird and wonderful, never-before-seen products in its catalogue pages.

This notoriety stirred Wella, the shampoo company, to request a meeting. They were interested to know how Cosmetics to Go came up with such creative ideas.

During the meeting, Mark began the discussion by getting to the very basics of the product-making process and asked the simple question,

❝ What is shampoo? ❞

Breaking it down to very basic levels, they discussed that to most manufacturers shampoo is just surfactant and water. You can thicken it with expensive chemical substances, or use common household ingredients such as salt as a thickener.

Mark seized upon this and began to enthuse about the possibilities of playing around with this humble ingredient. What might happen if more salt was added? Would different types of salt have different effects?

Whilst the Wella director sat politely and gamely joined in the discussion, it didn't seem to be lighting his fire and he seemed a little perplexed as to where all the chat was going.

Long after his visitor had left, Mark was still thinking about the idea and began experimenting in the labs with salt in all its variances, trying to find a fabulous saline formula to delight customers.

Eventually he discovered the perfect salt to shampoo ratio. This final formula was to become Serpentine Shampoo – a clear shampoo that smelt divine and gave hair a fabulous volumising boost! (Pertinently, years later this shampoo was to evolve and appear in a much saltier incarnation as Big in the Lush range.)

Once Serpentine had been delivered, the inventors went all out, taking inspiration from all the seashore had to offer. Kelp, carrageen and Irish moss seaweeds were all sourced from Peter Nolan, an Irish fisherman. These ingredients were to be included in their new range, Sea Level, which flourished!

Strandlooper

From prehistoric times up to the second millennium, the nomadic Strandlopers traversed the coastal regions of what is now Southwestern Africa. This indigenous group originating from the Khoikhoi people survived by hunting, foraging and gathering, making the most of resources they could glean from beachcombing along the shoreline.

While on a trip to Namibia, Rowena learned about an archeological dig where researchers had uncovered the graves of people believed to be Strandlopers. She was struck by the detail that each person was buried holding a shell in their hand. Touched by this story, she brought a shell back from her travels especially for Mark.

The team wanted to acknowledge the history of Strandloper people and were called to name their new ocean-inspired hair treatment after them, explaining: 'our hair and scalp conditioner is a collection of this and that from the seashore.' In its most elaborate formulation, Strandlooper contained twenty-six different ingredients and was a customer favourite. The success of this concept led to reformulations on the existing Sea Level products, which evolved to become known as the Strandlooper range.

Peter Nolan harvesting the seaweed

'Squelchy and lovely'
Melissa Harmes · London.

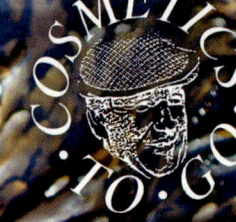

Pure Luxury

Describing the delights of Cosmetics to Go in *Tatler* magazine, journalist Susan Irving encouraged her readers to put on some rose-tinted spectacles, lie back and indulge. '*You are a Sybarite not a Spartan!*' was her rallying call to bathers everywhere. The Luxury range, full of truly pampering products, provided ample opportunity to do so.

Using any of this decadent selection would transport you into a romantic fairytale, complete with captivating fragrances to lose yourself in and soothing, silky textures to caress the skin.

Violet Nights Bath Oil, a best-selling favourite from the moment it was introduced, turned bath water a creamy milky white and left a fragrant trail of violet kisses up and down the bather's body. Once established, more violet-scented products would spring up around it, such as Aunty Vi's Cream Talc. This was a miraculous, oil-rich white cream that sank into the skin leaving a powdery talc to be smoothed off to reveal perfectly soft skin.

For those who preferred bubbles in their tubs, the sinfully indulgent Saucery, bursting with chocolatey goodness, was a firm favourite. This rich mixture contained oils from avocado, peach kernel, camellia and pumpkinseed to moisturise, but more importantly cocoa powder and a rich chocolate scent good enough to make your mouth water.

A love of chocolate was also responsible for the development of the delectable Knights in White Chocolate. Mark felt a sudden craving and, unable to resist, was compelled to jump on his bike and cycle to the local shop to pick some up. Riding back satiated and with a mouth full of chocolate, he began to think about the ingredients that went into his bar. Cocoa butter, cocoa and sugar made the confection, so why not experiment with the cocoa butter content and make a solid massage bar? Inspired, he leapt from his two-wheeler and off to the labs to experiment.

What emerged was the Knights in White Chocolate massage bar, the name inspired by the Moody Blues song, 'Knights in White Satin'. The massage bar came packaged in golden foil and looked for all the world like a mouth-wateringly tasty, selection-box chocolate. The inspiration for this came from seeing chocolates displayed so appealingly and elegantly in the Rococo Chocolates shop in the King's Road. When warmed, this bar melted onto your skin for a sweet, white chocolate massage experience. The first massage bar was born!

Following this success, and considering the popularity of the Violet Nights range, Violet Fondant Massage Bar came along next. This was a mouth-watering chocolate massage bar suffused with a violet leaf infusion. Cosmetics to Go really knew how to look after chocoholics!

For those of a showering disposition, Orchid Shower Gel and Lemon Melt were provided. Fresh dove orchid flower petals were mixed alongside a jasmine, mimosa and ylang ylang fragrance in the Orchid Shower Gel. The Lemon Melt was just as gooey and delicious to rub up and down your body. It contained a slice of fresh lemon peel for added citrus piquancy and grated cocoa butter that melted onto your skin for super moisturising softness.

Rose Tinted Spectacles Bubble Bath, the invention that had inspired the *Tatler* article, was a glorious symphony of rosewater and honey that became a luxurious rose-scented bathing experience. Once completely relaxed in the pink water and surrounded by foaming bubbles, subtle adagios of geranium and jasmine would gently whisper to you through the steam.

Companion to this was the Turkish Bath, a lavish, whipped mousse to be smothered on before bathing or showering and then gently massaged off once in the water. Pure bliss on the skin designed to leave you smelling delicious enough to nibble on. Rose lovers will be pleased to read that a version of this found its way into Lush, where it is called Turkish Delight.

Finally, before we leave the alluring charms of Cosmetics to Go's luxury range, we should mention the delightful Honey Buns. This moisturising bubble bath was made mostly of pure, clear honey and bubbled with the sweet scent of vanilla, beeswax and mimosa, allowing you to drift off in a honeyed haze.

> Lemon Melt - I got it for Christmas, and when I first used it, it was one of the most gooky, gooey, gorgeous and beautiful things I'd ever done - I felt very rich.
> J Hall - Chelmsford, Essex.

Pure Luxury | 113

The Ultimate Bathing Experience

Bathing by candlelight adds a sense of calm, magic and seduction and in time scented candles were introduced. Each candle's fragrance matched that of a product taken from the new-agey Serendipity range. Twilight's scent was designed to relax, 9 Lives Celtic evoked the smells of a forest in your bathroom and Despair was for those who wanted to wallow in sorrow as well as the bath.

Anthony Critchlow, a designer (and alumni of the band, Living In A Box), created enchanting candlestick holders that could be attached to the wall. He also designed bath racks adorned with the Cosmetics to Go cupids. Local blacksmiths from Dorset were charged to forge these in their fires, and the final design incorporated candlesticks, a bookstand and soap dishes for truly decadent bathing. For those who tippled while the bathwater rippled, there was also a combined candlestick and wine glass holder. How sublime!

The Serendipity Range

Steve 'Happy Hippy' Pierson

There was also a selection of supremely wacky shower caps! The Happy Hippy shower cap came complete with a loofah attached, so you could scrub as you showered. Even sillier was the shower cap with a foam microphone attached, so you could throw your best rock star poses as you sang in the shower.

For ultimate convenience, a shower capstan was invented – a nifty invention that you attached to your wall and slotted your shower gel bottle into. This clever little item let you swing the bottle upside down to dispense gel into your hand, and then it would flip itself back to an upright position, saving you precious liquid!

The Ultimate Bathing Experience

Neroli range - especially the Triple Orange Blossom Cream - I've never had a cream that does so many different jobs and smells gorgeous. It's multi-talented!!
R Richardson - Dunfermline, Fife.

ORANGE & SPICE AND ORANGE BLISS
An effective and unashamedly beautiful hand-crafted soap combined with a mild and creamy hair and body wash make up this specially selected set, allowing you to indulge yourself with this truly princely oil and pamper yourself quite literally from head to toe ! We were originally going to call this set 'Orange A Night With A Prince' but it never quite happened...

The Prince of Neroli range - The smells make me swoon!
N Ramsden - Bristol, Avon.

Summertime and the living was easy. The Prince of Neroli range provided a burst of sunshine straight into the bathroom.

The essential oil that lent the inspiration for this range was named after the legendary Princess of Nerola. She was famous for anointing herself, her baths and her gloves with neroli – the essence of bitter orange tree flowers.

Neroli is a perfumer's delight. It is sweetly floral, and has uplifting qualities to transport its wearer to a happy place. It's also a costly material. The delicate blossoms must be hand-picked from the tree, and it takes blossoms from around sixty trees just to produce one kilogramme of this precious essential oil. The Neroli range was a heavenly walk through orange groves on a summer's day.

The Prince of Neroli Cologne was a gentle, alcohol-free body splash. Once you had completed your toilette, you could adorn yourself with Neroli for Fragrant Hair, so when you walked into a room you could enrapture your audience with just a swish of the head.

The team also adored neroli for the rejuvenating and soothing properties that it has on the skin. They used this to great effect in perhaps the most beloved product to emerge from this range. Triple Orange Blossom Cream was a creamy, white shaving cream that gently allowed you to shave away whiskers whilst leaving skin soft, moisturised and smelling divine.

This remarkable cream attracted the attention of Andrew Gerrie, a dynamic young businessman who was looking for investment opportunities. He had fallen in love with Cosmetics to Go after using this product. He approached the team with a view to establishing the brand in Australia and New Zealand and although meetings were held, nothing materialised. Cosmetics to Go's operations remained UK only. This introduction, however, would pave the way for Andrew's involvement with members of the team in the not so distant future...

Neroli Hair Perfume - It's the fragrance I've been trying to track down for nearly 15 years! Reminds me of a really good year I spent in Spain. A very evocative scent.
K Redhead - Watford, Hertfordshire.

NEROLI COLOGNE AND HAIR PERFUME
A set of products that allows you to experience the power and presence of this most highly prized oil. Some of our customers describe the scent as 'evocative', others as 'heaven' and some go as far as 'totally addictive'. We would describe the fragrance as 'sweetly floral and uplifting' and that just leaves you to enjoy this pair of products and form your own conclusions.

Andrew Gerrie. CRIKEY they say in New Zealand.

Neroli | 117

Cosmetics to Go

DANGER! The Summer Sale

Inspired by an Alfred Hitchcock film poster, this cover was uncannily prescient as it featured the infamous Summer Sale of 1993 that would see the whole company brought to its knees.

Cosmetics to Go was carrying too much stock. Over the six years of its existence, range after range of new products had been introduced. Each time lines were discontinued old products, unwanted labels and abandoned packaging would sit unsold and defunct in a huge warehouse. A sale was needed so a test batch of special sale catalogues were sent to a select group of customers to gauge demand. Five per cent of these recipients bought and calculations were made as to how many catalogues would be needed to clear the stock. These were printed and posted.

At the same time a new promotion to attract customers was tried. Tickety Boo asked customers to supply the names of ten friends who hadn't used Cosmetics to Go before. Each would receive a free gift and their name would be put on the mailing list. The products offered were taken from the top ten items most often sent as gifts, so if a customer filled out all ten addresses Cosmetics to Go would send out free items to the amount of £25.

The Summer Sale was a huge success in getting those extra people ordering, but money was pouring out of the company and operations were cracking at the seams... twenty per cent of the recipients of the catalogue sent a cheque but the prices advertised were so low that there was no way to make a profit and Cosmetics to Go were swamped with vanloads of heavy mail sacks containing orders and cheques and lists of friends for freebies. Customers who couldn't believe the great deals inside were calling their friends and sharing the good news. Folk who had never bought from Cosmetics to Go before jumped in to reap the rewards of these exceptionally generous offers.

A customer named Hilary Jones called to chase an order and was informed that they simply did not have the staff available to sort through the deluge of correspondence. Hilary offered her services, and came down to help sift through the piles. She began going through copious amounts of post, separating out fan mail, complaints, Tickety Boos, cheques and orders into separate piles. It became her full-time job. Little did she know that this simple, helpful gesture would result in a long working relationship that would carry on into Lush.

The phone rooms were bombarded with callers eager to make the most of these bargains and the lines were jammed constantly. Staff were brought in to help answer the calls and process orders, as volumes were higher than ever previously experienced. The number of phone lines increased from eight to twelve and then twenty-four, and still these were not enough to handle the onslaught.

Liz remembers: 'We had a computer that could tell you when there was more calls coming in than available operators. I could see on the system when we had calls waiting, so we would get extra people to put on headsets. They'd jump in and nobody could tell that they had just been pulled in from another department or office.'

Danger!

Despite the phone room technology, Cosmetics to Go was not equipped for the unforeseen volumes of calls. Phone lines and computers would often go down, losing whole tranches of orders. When computer information was lost in a crash, there was no way to tell which customers had already been sent their order. Duplicate orders were issued just in case, and two sets of parcels would often arrive on the doorsteps of customers.

The sale was so successful that the factory ran clear out of sale stock and this meant they were making new products to sell at sale prices, way below any price that could have covered the cost of materials. The company was running at full steam and simply could not keep up with the crazy demand. They were forced to return unfulfilled orders and cheques. This left customers unhappy and dissatisfied.

Cosmetics to Go, always a workplace in a whirlwind of activity, battened down the hatches and took it up to gale force twelve. The offices and factories were hurricanes of staff frantically working day and night to keep up with demand, all at huge cost to the company. At one point Mark remembers realising every parcel they sent out was losing the company a pound.

The extra sales incurred extra costs. Everyone was working overtime to make products to match demand. Phone room operators had dealt with relentless calls and the tiny satellite companies who Cosmetics to Go hired to help were suddenly called on to triple output and increase production too. Compounding the losses was the very large bill from the Post Office.

The Post Office had their own problems, having had a series of wildcat strikes – just what wasn't needed. Arguments (and relations) between Cosmetics to Go and the Post Office got nasty.

Mark and Alan working hard

From the very beginning, Cosmetics to Go had been unique as a mail-order company because they didn't charge customers for postage. Things were not looking good. Between 1990 and 1992, Britain was in a deep recession, starting with a housing crisis. Lloyds Bank was lending Constantine & Weir £2 million and the normal polite meetings changed. The local manager retired and the regional manager also disappeared and a far less amenable banker arrived as Lloyds Bank reacted to the economic cycle and began calling in its loans.

The company had expanded from a simple manufacturing business into a complicated beast that involved retailing, mail order and manufacturing. In the whirlwind of starting up a new company and the ensuing speed of light at which they had conducted operations, keeping hold of the cash had become much more difficult. The final tranche payment of £3 million from the Body Shop agreement for ownership of product formulas was still owed. The bank withdrew its facility at the same time as some of this money came in and cash became tight.

DANGER! The Summer Sale | 121

What Next?

Searching for a Saviour...

Although efforts were being made to stem the tide of money flowing from the business, in the winter of 1993, the directors realised that they were going to need help. There was no money in the coffers. Cosmetics to Go needed a cash injection and finding an investor had become an urgent task. In November, a meeting was arranged in London with potential investor Andrew Varley, a director of Next.

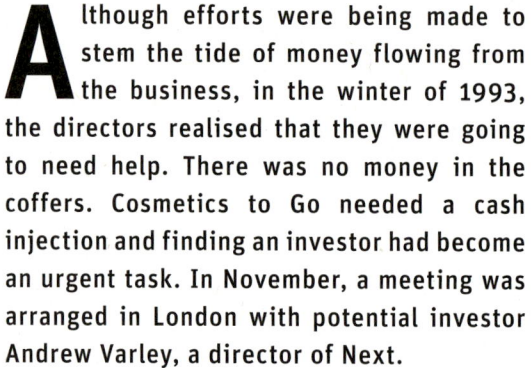

Andrew liked what he was presented with and was willing to recommend that his fellow directors at Next take a closer look at the business. This seemed like a good match as Next was a well-known name in the UK, firmly established in the catalogue business and, most importantly, had the capital to get Cosmetics to Go onto a firm footing financially.

Plans were made to visit the business in Poole. The Cosmetics to Go team were slightly nonplussed when Next called ahead to check if there was a suitable spot nearby to land their helicopter, and a Next director was duly despatched to come down and see how the company operated. After this director was given a tour of the properties, shown through the books, and had discussions about the state of the business and its potential, a dinner was arranged for Karl and Mark to meet with David Jones, Next's Managing Director, in Leicester. Here a handshake agreement was made not to discuss a sale with anyone else. In principle, Next was on board. The Cosmetics to Go team breathed a sigh of relief and started drafting up an agreement.

122 | Cosmetics to Go

The Dream Team

What a show stopper!

The Final Clothes Show

The third and final year that Cosmetics to Go exhibited at *The Clothes Show Live* was emotionally charged. Behind the scenes, nerves and pressure were mounting. This event was important and needed to be a roaring success to boost confidence and woo potential investors to the Cosmetics to Go brand. At the same time, it demonstrated an insouciant exercise in extravagance, with a stand that echoed the homes of the Gods themselves, Olympus.

All the staff who went to work at the show were aware that money was tight and viewed this as an opportunity to show off not only their unique range and products, but also to make the company look great and to keep customer confidence too.

The stand was busy and beautiful, but the recession had reached a point where unemployment had risen by over fifty per cent, from around seven per cent in 1990 to almost eleven per cent of the population in 1993. It was glumly noted that many visitors were most enthusiastic for freebies.

Helen on duty

Mark polishing his wings

In the stand

The tiredness sets in

What Next? & The Final Clothes Show | 123

A Christmas Present

Christmas came, and having got through the sale things worked out a little better. In busy periods Cosmetics to Go operated a 24/7 operation, with the factory turning over products in two ever-looping shifts and a chattering phone room answering calls night and day. The only time of the year where the offices lay silent and ponderous in the absence of humans cluttering up the place was on Christmas Day.

Up in the staff room on the very top floor, a broken radiator was disconnected from the system and propped up against a wall ready to be replaced. Innocuously enough it sat there.

To save money, if only for one day, the heating was turned off. As the temperature fell that night, for the first time in months this little top room became cold enough to open the thermostat and the system started to pump.

It was late in the evening of Christmas Day when Mark received a phone call from the Dorset Constabulary informing him that the alarm was sounding at the Cosmetics to Go offices and that water had been seen seeping out of the building under the front door. He rallied Steve, who had been enjoying festivities at a colleague's house, and they roused themselves to meet Mark on site.

The site of the flood, Cosmetics to Go, Jolliffe House, Poole

Arriving at the property, they sloshed through the sizeable puddle that had formed outside the entrance. Tentatively opening the door they were hit by the smell of ozone in the air and a wave of water. With a sinking feeling they surveyed the devastation. The nearby ceiling had collapsed under the weight of water and an indoor waterfall was running down the walls. Electrical crackles and sparks of light arced in the air. The office furniture resembled sad islands marooned in a dirty brown ocean, where all kinds of flotsam and jetsam drifted around in listless swirls.

As they went through each room paperwork floated sadly atop the water, invoices and letters were inky blurs, photographs all drifted in mournful circles. Posters had curled and fallen damply from the walls.

The filing cabinets were still locked up but couldn't prevent the water from seeping in. Normally the Cosmetics to Go offices were bursting with personality and fun, but now all the personal touches were sodden and ruined. The computers were done for, the documents were all pulpy wads and even cuddly desk mascots had been drenched and dirtied beyond saving.

Tentatively and grimacing, they sloshed up the stairs to the second floor, and solemnly reviewed a painfully similar sight – a second water-destroyed phone room and water pouring from the ceiling above. Looking at each other in disbelief they ascended to the third floor. More water everywhere, and this was where they could see the unbelievable culprit, a tiny pipe that had innocuously ruined an entire building. Finally, at the site of the crime they turned the water off and stood in the damp listening to the drip-drip-drip...

The whole building was a write off. Damp and dispirited they made their way back down the watery staircase, gloomily inspecting ruined rooms and equipment. Looking at each other they slipped out of the front door and quietly closed it behind them. It was the beginning of the end.

A Christmas Present

COSMETICS TO GO HAVE GONE

When the end came it came swiftly. The news came through that Next had changed their minds and would not be investing in the company. They decided to pull out and all hope was lost with this unexpected about-turn.

Why did Next pull out? In David Jones' biography *Next to Me* he wrote:

'We were invited and foolishly accepted the invitation – to become the British end of an American venture called Bath & Body Works, a version of The Body Shop launched by The Limited, the huge US retail group founded by Les Wexner. David Wolfson and I visited The Limited's headquarters in Columbus, Ohio, several times...

We opened five Bath & Body Works stores in the UK in the autumn of 1994, but the whole experiment was doomed to failure. We had to overprice the product because of import duty, and the sales per square foot were not high enough to cover the much higher rent charged in the UK compared with US stores...

We struggled to make it work and Mr Wexner began to get irritated with us. When The Limited decided to float Bath & Body Works as a separate company, we took the opportunity to come out of the joint venture...'

There was no money left and no way to get hold of any. On advice from a firm of receivers, and with huge regret after seventeen years of business, Constantine & Weir aka Cosmetics to Go were forced to go into administration on 17 January 1994.

The directors were immediately in the unenviable position of being unable to control the dismantling of their company or the fees piling up, but having to witness it. A liquidation auction was announced and became the talk of the town. Many Poole locals had ties to the business. Even if they personally had not been a Cosmetics to Go employee or customer, there was a good chance that they had a relative or friend who had been.

Steve Brackstone recalls Liz Weir going for a walk on Poole Quay with Mark and coming back to announce that she was no longer employed. Pretty disconcerting news as Liz was his boss at the time.

Jason Muller, who along with his brothers had worked in the business since school, recalls rumours in the factory about the company winding down, 'When you are involved in that, you're talking about a family business with things going on, you're going to hear things. So people were aware.' Word was trickling out. Jason was one of the first to be called to the office and one of the first to go. That day fifteen people were let go from the factory.

Alan Hopking remembers hearing the news whilst on a visit to the factory. He had recently delivered a consignment of aloe and dashed to recover it, but was informed that he could not have it back. Now all the property of Cosmetics to Go belonged to the receivers. He cursed them and left.

On the day of the auction, when everything in the factory was to be sold off, the road leading to it was packed solid with cars. Jeff Osment had come to the auction to bid for the TV monitor from the lab and a couple of bits and pieces. He noticed that quite a lot of items that should have been there were missing. All of the technical equipment he had bought for the cinema had disappeared.

With the doors to Cosmetics to Go shut, the team members had no option but to scatter to the winds. The whole process happened so quickly that most people were left in shock, suddenly faced with decisions about what to do in order to get new jobs as quickly as they could.

The story of the collapse of Cosmetics to Go spread quickly through the local community and Directors were sometimes approached by members of the public who would catch up with them in town and ask them what had happened. Paul remembers the mum of an ex-employee berating him in a car park.

Bournemouth Evening Echo, 22 April 1994

Your wish is granted.

Right at the end of the winding down, when Helen was given her redundancy notice, she took a final Blackberry Bath Bomb to use. Once home she ran a bath, threw it into the tub and was about to step in when she noticed something unusual. The piece of paper that was hidden at the heart of the bath bomb and normally read BOOM! had floated to the surface of the water, but it said something very different…

Helen had no idea how this message had got inside this particular bath bomb, but the words and the sentiment stopped her in her tracks. All of a sudden, she felt a relief, as if a great weight had been lifted from her shoulders. The beloved Cosmetics to Go was sadly no more and had been painfully taken away, but it did mean an awful lot of the stress and panic of trying to rein in the runaway company was lifted.

Suddenly there was space, and quiet and a chance to realign and decide what was going to happen next…

Seventeen years later, Helen still keeps this fragile slip of paper in a jewellery box. It reminds her of an extremely painful time, but also reminds her how even a traumatic ending can lead to new adventures and beginnings…

Helen's jewellery box

Farewell to a place of beauty

COSMETICS-To-Go – the brilliant, wacky, Poole-based beauty firm has gone.

I loved their daft ideas, my husband loves their shampoo, and where we'll get a comparable nappy cream for my son Zak now, God only knows.

What I do know is this, that something is going badly wrong when such an excellent outfit such as CTG goes down the tubes.

Mark Constantine and Liz Weir — I know you must be gutted by what's happened to your firm, but please don't lose heart.

And, if it's at all possible, please don't give up the idea of trying something as brave, bold and principled as was CTG, in the future.

The brilliant and wacky Cosmetics-To-Go has gone – it will be sorely missed

Bournemouth Echo, 25 April 1994 by Faith Eckersall

The Grand Finale: Fizz, Fireworks & Friends

Although Cosmetics to Go sadly came to an end, the story would continue.

In 1995, Mark and Mo Constantine, Liz Bennett, Rowena Bird, Helen Ambrosen and Paul Greeves reunited to start a new company, Lush Cosmetics.

They returned to the very same building on Poole High Street that had housed Cosmetics to Go and opened up the very first Lush shop. Lush is now a thriving business with over 850 shops in over 52 different countries.

It was at a Lush managers' meeting in 2011 that Matt (Lush Books Publisher) and Mira (Lush editor and writer) first sat down with Mark to discuss writing a book about Lush. He was leafing through some suggestions we had presented to him, when it became obvious that another idea had occurred to him.

'It seems to me,' he declared, 'that you can't write a book about Lush without writing a book about Cosmetics to Go first.'

With that our course was set. We began in earnest. We started unearthing documents and products from dusty long-forgotten archives. We travelled all over Dorset and beyond to interview as many people connected to Cosmetics to Go as possible.

After months of research and reminiscing, this book was born.

Early on in the project, Mark was once again looking at our work, this time at some design concepts we were presenting. They just weren't hitting the spot. He compared our work to a selection of vibrant Cosmetics to Go catalogues and it was immediately obvious that we needed to buck our ideas up. We had a lot to live up to!

Mark suggested that we ask Clive Holmes and his company CHS Studios to help. After all, they had designed the catalogues, logos, labels and the look of pretty much everything for Cosmetics to Go. Who better than Clive to guide us?

Clive and his team were a little surprised to hear from us but invited us to their offices in Christchurch to find out what we were up to. The parting of ways at the end of Cosmetics to Go had been difficult. Fortunately, any hesitation was quashed after they heard about our mission to create a book. Clive and his team's expertise and experience were crucial for the book's success, and we were thrilled when they agreed to work with us.

Over the course of the project, Clive and his team went to great lengths to help us capture the essence of the classic Cosmetics to Go catalogues in book form. Without their assistance and guidance, this book would not have been possible.

We found and tracked down many ex-employees, partners and customers of Cosmetics to Go. People kindly granted us hours of their time reminiscing. Some

ascended into lofts and excavated sheds to find us treasured relics they had held onto. Others connected us to long-lost interviewees that we would never have found by ourselves, and we were offered endless cups of tea as we gathered stories and anecdotes. Conversations evoked all kinds of sentimental memories, some that made us laugh, and some that left us in tears. This book was built on these recollections and acts of kindness.

Once the book was completed we invited everyone who had helped to celebrate with us. Rachel Constantine, event planner extraordinaire, and Jo Armitage, expert designer and stylist, were brought in to help us create something special. The party was to be held at the Italian Villa in Compton Acres Gardens in Poole. This glorious 1920s venue is more accustomed to hosting weddings, but for one night only it was transformed to take attendees back in time for a Cosmetics to Go celebration. Those on the guest list received their invitation in an authentic-looking CTG parcel complete with stickers.

CTG party invite ready to go

The Grand Finale | 131

No detail was spared. Flowers for each table setting were displayed in Dr. Martens boots inspired by the Don't Bovver With Boots CTG catalogue cover, a delivery bike complete with its basket full of parcels stood proudly on display, a wall was decorated with pictures of CTG employees, a magical fairground carousel shone as it spun around outside in the car park. There was even a full band to keep celebrations going after the sit-down dinner and a fireworks display to end the evening.

Rachel remembers: 'I particularly loved wrapping all the parcels with stickers we had created. We designed them to replicate exactly what CTG used to do, and that was really good fun.'

She was aware of the responsibility of the assignment. 'I knew that it was a very creative but very delicate thing to get involved with,' she confides. 'The Constantine family had spoken about the tragedy of losing the company and how awful it was. We wanted to make sure that the party was a celebration of all of the best bits of Cosmetics to Go; the artwork, all of the amazing products, big flowers, nice food and we had a carousel! It was about trying to create happy memories for the attendees, and of course the founders.'

The guest list was bursting with Cosmetics to Go employees, most of CHS and lots of Lush staff. Almost everybody that had agreed to be interviewed or helped behind the scenes made an appearance.

The guest of honour was Faith Eckersall, the journalist who had written and published the kind tribute to Cosmetics to Go in the *Bournemouth Echo Newspaper* (see page 129). Mark credits Faith with inspiring the team to pick themselves up and try again.

For Clive and Mark, it was the first time that they had met since they had last worked together. The room audibly buzzed happily on observing them shake hands, share a greeting and a roar of laughter.

Don't bovver with boots

Mark & Clive in the photobooth

Mo, Helen & Karl out for a spin

Clive & Ro celebrate the launch of the Cosmetics to Go book

As the night went on, the room broke into ever-changing groups as past co-workers, suppliers, friends and family mingled, caught up, reunited and danced the night away.

It was a night of laughter, rekindled friendships, and an acknowledgment of the time spent at Cosmetics to Go.

Rowena recalls:

'It was nice seeing faces from the past. Everybody was very friendly. Although the ending of the business was painful and people were upset with us, they still came together to celebrate the four years that we'd had at Cosmetics to Go.'

Helen admitted to feeling a little nervous about attending the event. These feelings lifted at the party though. She particularly enjoyed reconnecting with Alan Hopking, the herbalist, who had been a big influence in her product creation. 'I loved seeing Alan,' she reminisced. 'When we worked together he told me "you're a wizard!" I thought, that's amazing because I think you're a warlock! It was great to catch up with him and tell him that we were still using his work.'

She also loved the brightly lit carousel in the car park.

'It was just really lovely riding on that roundabout, seeing everybody together: I was very nervous about the party but it was lovely and it was a good thing to do. I remember good things about it and it felt better afterwards. It felt like a release.'

The Grand Finale | 133

The Grand Finale | 135

The Cosmetics to Go book and celebratory party reignited old bonds and friendships. They were remembered, renewed and in some cases reforged in Lush.

John Thain, a consultant who had advised the CTG team on marketing, would go on to work with Jack Constantine, our Head of Lush Digital, for a while. Janis Paskin, who first worked in PR for Cosmetics to Go, re-joined Lush in 2019 as a Brand Guardian and Non-Executive Director.

Julie Rogers, who worked at Cosmetics to Go and is currently the archivist at Lush, also attended the party. 'It was nice to see some of the gang there who I hadn't seen for years. We were talking about the old times which actually only feels like yesterday!'

Julie catching up with old friends

As well as bringing people together, the book and party served to heal painful feelings of heartbreak, loss and shame around the demise of the business. There was a sea change in how 'the company that came before Lush' was regarded. Lush could begin to celebrate all the wonderful things that it had achieved and recognise its influence.

As the Lush Archivist and one of the longest-standing members of staff, Julie has a unique view of the whole timeline. Hired by Mark as a teenager fresh to the world of work in 1981, Julie has witnessed some of our best-selling Lush products evolve from Cosmetics to Go favourites.

'Cosmetics to Go was bursting with product inspiration and this is true of Lush too. No idea is a bad idea – they all get a chance,' she says. 'A lot of products released by Lush came from CTG.'

Karl Bygrave also remarked on how the creativity of those few years are still inspiring Lush's latest ranges decades later. 'Recently, the Sea Level range of products influenced our latest hair care products, with Swell and Squeak shampoos utilising sea salt to brilliant effect,' he informs, 'and Salarium perfume returned as a fine fragrance and body spray.'

'We can't forget that some of our global best sellers started in Cosmetics to Go,' he adds, and points to Mask of Magnaminty face and body mask, one of Lush's most successful products, which began its life as Mydvvai. (see page 50)

'Product-wise, Cosmetics to Go had a massive impact,' remarks Mo. 'Even now, local colleges and universities study the business and Cosmetics to Go catalogues.

'It's interesting working with the next generation who have never heard of Cosmetics to Go,' she muses. 'They had never seen anything like it. Now they're exploring and exclaiming, "Look at all these things!"'

She laughs, thinking of the product meetings where Lush inventors come together to show off what they have been working on. 'I wonder how many times I have seen my own creations presented by colleagues? "Great idea. Oh, yeah, we've done all that already at CTG!"'

IT'S NOT JUST THE PRODUCTS THAT HAVE FILTERED THROUGH TO LUSH

'I recently unearthed an early version of the 10 Rules of CTG' (see pages 86–87) Julie explains. 'It obviously was a foundation for Lush's We Believe statement.' Karl still refers to his very old copy of the 10 Rules of Lush from time to time.

Helen commented that everyone who worked at Cosmetics to Go brought lessons from their time there into Lush. 'We used to buy finished fragrances for our products but when ranges were discontinued we were left with large amounts of perfume that would never get used.' she observed. 'Lush makes its own fragrance and in batches forecast to match production.'

'Cosmetics to Go always had problems with overstocking,' she says. 'When Lush started, this led to the development of a business model emphasising fresh, made-to-order products. These approaches have helped Lush maintain flexibility, reduce waste, and improve cost efficiency.'

One of the challenges experienced at Cosmetics to Go was overspending on packaging that quickly became unusable as ranges were often updated or completely discontinued. This left the business stuck with cupboards full of unusable materials. At Lush, a main goal is to focus on developing 'naked products' that need no packaging at all. Shampoo bars (as seen on pages 34–35) are displayed in colourful stacks in Lush shops with not a wisp of foil between them.

The impact of Cosmetics to Go's successes and challenges, from creative inspiration to business strategies and ethical goals, is embedded in Lush's DNA.

After the echoes of this book's launch party's final fireworks faded, carriages arrived to whisk attendees off to their homes, leaving behind an empty venue and a sense of closure. The displays and pictures were carefully taken down and can be seen in all their glory at the Lush Archive on the Nuffield Estate in Poole along with lots of other recovered Cosmetics to Go treasures.

The book and the party didn't just commemorate the past, they redefined how Cosmetics to Go was perceived within the Lush community.

The renewed pride and confidence around the Cosmetics to Go legacy became evident as Lush embraced and celebrated its origins with its first-ever subscription box, launched in April 2014. It was introduced with great fanfare and contained classic Cosmetics to Go products Violet Nights bath oil, Lemon Melt shower gel (see page 112) and Super Tramp shower gel – an updated version of the classic Smaragadine formula (see page 51).

Cosmetics to Go products and inspirations still filter through into our ranges, and the lessons learned will never be forgotten. Mark points out: 'Looking back, Cosmetics to Go has turned into Mary Poppins' carpet bag. You know, the one she pulls a standard lamp out of. Every time we face a challenge at Lush, there is something learned that we can draw from, be it from a product formula, a stunning image, or a quote that is appropriate to the situation. I also recognise it as a very stressful lesson. Neither Body Shop nor Lush asked for so much out of everyone, but wow, it still shines with that light today. When I reflect, every decision we make at Lush today has its guts in Cosmetics to Go.'

Rowena's reflection captures the sentiment best: 'Although I feel close to tears about Cosmetics to Go ending, you can't really be sad that it went because Lush came out of it, and who wouldn't want Lush?'

Closing up shop

138 | Cosmetics to Go

A new beginning...?

TO BE CONTINUED...

Credits

Illustrations

All illustrations by Cosmetics to Go, except:

Endpapers Sally Holland

P14	Dastardly Daphne		P62–63	Dastardly Daphne
P18–19	Dastardly Daphne		P70	Molly Morris
P21	Molly Moris		P74–75	Molly Morris
P24–27	Sally Holland		P86–87	Adam Taylor
P28	Cherub by Dastardly Daphne		P92–93	Dastardly Daphne
P35	Molly Morris		P96–97	Martin Bachell
P40–41	Molly Morris		P104	Lush Shop by Adam Taylor

Photos

All photos by Cosmetics to Go, except:

P12	Dave Blunden
P15	Richard Skins/Lush Limited
P16	Mark & Anita by Charlie Stebbings
P23	Katie Foulkes/Lush Limited
P24	Mark & Mo Constantine
P28–29	Rowena Bird
P34	Mark & Mo Constantine
P36	Mark & Mo Constantine
P54	Office by CHS creative
P55	Rooftop by CHS creative
P56	Steve Pierson by CHS creative
P61	Customers by Cosmetics to Go customers
Helen & Robin from Helen Ambrosen
Rowena from Rowena Bird
P62	Helen & Robin from Helen Ambrosen
P66–67	Dave Blunden
Jeff by Jeff Osment
Stills taken from Smelly-Vision produced by Jeff Osment
P76	Mark in Shirt by Mo Constantine
P78	Wesley by Clare Heyting
P80–81	Customers by Cosmetics to Go customers
Frame by Katie Foulkes/Lush Limited
P84–85	Rowena Bird CHS Creative
P88–89	Christmas Breakfast by Rowena Bird
P92	Tony Sanders, Ashley and Ann Rogers screenshots from CTG News produced by Jeff Osment
P98–99	*The Clothes Show Live* by BBC
P100	Video stack by CHS Creative
Screenshots from BBC, ITV, Wire TV
P101	Rowena on *The Big Breakfast* by Channel 4
P106–107	Rowena Bird
P109	Mark Constantine
P110	Seaweed by Greg Funnell
P117	Andrew Gerrie by Lush Ltd
P119	Hilary by Hippy Dave
P121	Rowena Bird
P123	Rowena Bird
P124	Richard Skins/Lush Limited
P128	Richard Skins/Lush Limited
P131	Sam Flynn/Lush Limited
P132	Tim Churchill
P133	Rachel Constantine & Rowena Bird
P134–135	Rachel Constantine & Tim Churchill
P136	Tim Churchill
P137	Cosmetic Warriors Ltd

Thank you

The idea for this book was first discussed on 14 November 2011, in the lounge of the Haven Hotel, Sandbanks. From that point onwards a cast of wise, generous and giving contributors supported us every step of the way. This is where we say thank you to all those good people, without whom this book would not exist.

Thank You

To the founders and directors of Cosmetics to Go, who worked and lived it, and then shared their personal memories and stories with us, so we could share it with you. Thank you so much to Mark Constantine, Mo Constantine, Liz Bennett, Rowena Bird, Helen Ambrosen and Karl Bygrave.

Our Lush colleagues who shared their memories of working at Cosmetics to Go with us; Steve Brackstone, Wesley Burrage, Sharon Etherington, Andrew Gerrie, Paul Greeves, Maxine James, Hilary Jones, Jason Muller and Julie Rogers.

The Cosmetics to Go employees that graciously allowed us to track them down and interview them, Chris Flynn, Marcia Harrison, Mark Bethell, Peter Woodward, John Thain, Martin Batchell, Alan Hopking and Janis Raven.

Our supportive colleagues at Carnaby Street, Strand Street, Lagland Street and the Market Street offices. You are the best cheerleaders ever. Thank you all.

Our ridiculously talented illustrators Dastardly Daphne, Stewart Harvey, Molly Morris, Dan Parkinson and Adam Taylor.

Clive Holmes, Steve Cotterill, Ian Charman, Tony Wilkes, Natasha Swarbrick, Steve Pierson, Dave Eaton and all at CHS Creative for design excellence and unwavering patience in the face of ever changing deadlines and lists of demands. We must mention Nicky Gover too – it was short but sweet!

Julia Lawrence for artworking this new edition of the book and for designing its new covers. Lily Thomas for looking after this book's original design files.

Jeff Osment for letting us raid his well-stocked film archives.

Simon, Jack and Claire Constantine for sharing their childhood memories.

Poole Museum for helping us find local newspaper cuttings and letting us work there undisturbed for hours at a time. All at Corkers, The Antelope and Pineview Guesthouse for emptying their garrets for this writer and giving me a home from home.

Andrew from Ashley Colour Laboratories for taking such good care of our precious images.

Noriko Miura and Shakira Roberts for recreating original Cosmetics to Go formulas for us to try.

Pat Shalhoub for taking time to reminisce with us about Jeff Brown.

Sam Flynn, Richard Skins and Pawel Winnicki, our photographers, who helped us out even when they were swamped. Tim Churchill for capturing the Cosmetics to Go reunion in photos at this book's launch party.

All the Lush forumites and old Cosmetics to Go customers who contributed memories, stories, offered support, help and enthusiasm. An honourable mention to Lush.a.lot who is kind of our unofficial archivist and always knowledgeable.

Charlotte Howe, for guiding us through catalogues and never being too busy to be beautiful with us, Kate Geary for her design eye and printer patience, Hannah D for her Sherlock Holmes skills and Sarah McCartney for her wedding memories.

Lisa Dickinson for giving me that gorgeous gloss!

Michelle Ashton, who helped put our first ideas together ensuring we got the gig at that fateful meeting.

The mystery benefactor who kept providing boxes of Cosmetics to Go treasures whenever we were hitting dead ends. We still don't know who you are but thank you!

Rachel Constantine and Jo Armitage for throwing us a fabulous party.

Thanks to our global LUSH colleagues who helped in the production of this book.

Helen Gould for her invaluable input.

Gina Wheatley for her support, meticulous fact checking, proofreading and insightful suggestions throughout.

Special thanks to Caitlin Doyle and Mary Thompson of HarperCollins.

Matt Fairhall would like to thank Darcie for her patience and listening skills in the early hours of the morning.

Mira Manga would like to personally thank:

Matt Fairhall for being a constant believer, keeping this ship's course steady and throwing down the anchor when we headed too close to the typhoons.

My lovely mum Chandra, nieces Teagan, Orlaith and Imogen and their awesome parents John Paul and Sinead.

Tom, thank you for being there. So much love to Sam, Kim & Jess – the three musketeers! My dear friend Amanda and the LA support crew, Paul and Tamie.

Tommy, thanks for being Tommy.